ALL SOULS IN MY TIME

ALL SOULS
IN MY TIME

A.L. Rowse

Emeritus Fellow of All Souls College, Oxford
Fellow of the British Academy
Fellow of the Royal Society of Literature

Duckworth

First published in 1993 by
Gerald Duckworth & Co. Ltd.
The Old Piano Factory
48 Hoxton Square, London N1 6PB
Tel: 071 729 5986
Fax: 071 729 0015

A catalogue record for this book is available
from the British Library

ISBN 0 7156 2474 1

The publishers are grateful to Hulton Deutsch for
supplying and giving permission to reproduce plates
5–8 and 13; to the Librarian of All Souls College, Oxford
and his staff for their help in supplying prints for
plates 1–4, 9–12 and 14–16, and to the Warden and
Fellows of All Souls for permission to reproduce them.

Photoset in North Wales by
Derek Doyle & Associates, Mold, Clwyd
Printed in Great Britain by
Biddles Ltd, Guildford and King's Lynn

Contents

Plates

between pages 124 and 125

Preface

I am primarily indebted to my publisher, Colin Haycraft – a fellow-Oxonian from the neighbouring college of Queen's – for suggesting that I write this book, but for whom I should not have thought of it. All Souls is frequently referred to in the public prints, but without much understanding of the nature of that peculiar institution. People seem unable to get it quite right. And indeed it must be admitted that it is impossible for anyone who has not lived within its walls to get the tone and temper of the life within it.

Of course it would be possible to write a heavy-weight history of the College in the twentieth century, from the documents and papers, books and memoirs. But that has not been my purpose. I have not even consulted the Diary and Journals I kept in College, indeed for most of my life at home and abroad. (I leave that to others, for the fun of a Boswell-type industry in the next century.) That would have made the book indeed *too* personal! Here I have relied on my memory.

Earlier this century it was difficult for outsiders – especially Americans and foreigners – to come to terms with a college without students. And in the later nineteenth and early twentieth century many 'reformers' proposed to transform All Souls or 'reform' it out of existence.

Today we are familiar with the idea of graduate colleges. Ironically, later this century several graduate colleges have been founded at both Oxford and Cambridge. I am old enough to remember the visit paid to us between the two

German wars by that noted American educationist, Abraham Flexner. Provided with the endowment to start up yet another university, he came over to study the working and purpose of All Souls – and went back to found something comparable, in the famous Institute for Advanced Studies at Princeton.

At the end of this book I have ventured to include, in an Appendix, a few poems, as some indication of a private inner life lived there, as against the outer life of research and tutoring, lecturing, examining and public affairs. The essence of the old College, which I loved, was to be a bridge between academic and public life, with mutual benefit to both. It would be a grievous mistake, an unimaginative impoverishment, to turn unique All Souls into yet one more ordinary academic institution.

New Year 1993   A.L.R.

CHAPTER 1

The Twenties

Many years ago, when I first came into College (in 1925), an American lady came into the front quad and, looking down into the crypt below the Chapel, where we then kept the coal, inquired kindly, 'Say, are these old ruins inhabited?' Since those good old days the crypt has been emptied, refurbished, lighted up to make lecture-rooms for under-graduates. I suppose that is a good thing, what is called progress.

In those days All Souls was rather empty during the week, speaking more to the imagination and of the past, filling up at weekends, and for College meetings and gaudies (at Cambridge, 'feasts'). In the two quadrangles and the little back Kitchen Quad, there was not all that much space for rooms. The College had been built for forty Fellows – now uncomfortably crowded for sixty-five or more. Too many – as with all colleges, for everybody in these equalitarian days wants to crowd into a college to share in its amenities, whether up to it or no. In such an age, under such a dispensation, colleges lose something of their *cachet*, and much of their charm.

Fortunately, I am to write only of the more congenial past, all that I care chiefly for.

Everybody seems to be mystified by the character and nature of All Souls, and few there are in the newsprints that get it right. But then they know no history.

The Colleges of Oxford and Cambridge are products of

the later Middle Ages. They were small institutions intended for graduates, not for undergraduates, who milled around the town in the carefree way of modern universities. Disciplinarian Tudor society brought them into the colleges to regularise their lives and teach them properly.

Strangely this did not happen at All Souls. Mainly because one-third of the Fellows were lawyers; these were found useful in public service, in various capacities as ambassadors and secretaries of state – and thus were given leave of absence on their missions. It is interesting historically, tribute to the useful traditionalism of English life, that this function has survived into our own time. A considerable number of our Fellows – the more varied and interesting section of the College (we academics were apt to call them the 'Londoners') – served the state or, to a lesser extent, the Church, at home or abroad in useful and congenial ways.

The stay-at-home Fellows, clerics and, to a lesser extent, academics, formed the larger number – less interesting to the historian. They *recur*, as a superior historian of neighbouring New College, H.A.L. Fisher, referred to undergraduates.

Thus, somehow, All Souls escaped recruiting undergraduates into its fellowship – no room for them anyway. We had only four of the sort, Bible Clerks, to help with the Chapel services. These had been reformed out of existence just before my advent. They were an anomaly, Chapel services were no longer what they had been, and we needed their rooms. I remember one or two of these rare birds coming back to visit us, one of them reproachfully thinking he ought to have been a Fellow (he wasn't up to it). Another, a good French scholar, H.J. Chaytor, became Head of a Cambridge college.

How then were the Fellows elected?

Before the reforming days of the nineteenth century,

largely from Founder's Kin, as with other colleges – notably New College, from which All Souls had been founded, by Archbishop Chichele in the 1430s. If one wants to see how this operated, the interior domestic life of New College, for example, read the soothing Diary of Parson Woodford. Would there had been a similar diary for All Souls! (There exists mine for our time, the twentieth century.)

New College was stuffed with Founder's Kin, as we were, and a very ordinary lot they mostly were. The All Souls lot were traditionally described as *bene nati, bene vestiti, mediocriter docti*, well born, well dressed, of middling learning. They were nearly all sons of country gentlemen or clergymen. Even in this century, one of these old fogies, asked how he had come up from the country, said, 'I hacked up from Waw-wickshire.' All the same, All Souls was exceptional in eighteenth-century Oxford in not being Tory: we were dominantly Whig. We could not have been favoured by my favourite Dr Johnson, though he did say, 'Sir, if a man has a mind to *prance* he must study at Christ Church and All Souls.'

Even in the later nineteenth century and up to the first German war, 1914-1918, the College was not Tory. Its inflexion was Whiggish, until Gladstone's Home Rule for Ireland produced the Liberal–Unionist defection. Of this group the constitutional lawyer A.V. Dicey was a proponent. G.M. Trevelyan told me that this group regarded the G.O.M. as 'phony' – which he was. (He was right about Ireland, however.)

This did not prevent the College from making the historic figure an Honorary Fellow – with a greater sense of justice and impartiality than Oxford has shown today towards another historic figure among its members.

As for Founder's Kin, I like to think that we have one today in William Waldegrave, though he arrived within our walls on his own merit, not on account of his ancestry, appealing as that is to an historian.

Since the reforming University Commissions of the nineteenth century our Prize Fellows, the main category, have been elected on the basis of an examination. There are other categories, professorial and research Fellows, which have become somewhat swollen latterly, though the Prize Fellows are the real thing.

The examination is held every October, and is a gruelling affair. Competitors enter from the other colleges – no point unless one had already got a First in the Schools, or a university prize, perhaps both. So, being elected is no matter of privilege – as some people would like to think (They should try sitting the examination!) – but of stiff competition.

As an accompaniment to the proceedings before election candidates are dined in Hall one by one. This was an ordeal I could well have done without. I had never dined at high table before, and I forget which of my friends at the House lent me the equipment to appear in. In those days full evening dress – tails and white tie – was the rule for guests. The ancient folklore was sufficiently discouraging: it was said that cherry-pie appeared on the menu, to see what the candidates did with the stones. One candidate passed the test perfectly by swallowing them, but he did not survive to be elected.

Oddly enough cherry-pie did appear on the night I dined. I was the guest of the Warden – too innocent to guess that that meant I was in the running. Opposite me sat the mummified figure of the Senior Fellow, so totally deaf as to be incommunicable, not a word was spoken by or to him. This was Sir Thomas Holland, an eminent lawyer whose portrait became familiar, up on the grand staircase of the Athenaeum, to which I was elected years later under their special Rule II. Warden Pember did his best to put me at my ease by opening up on Cornwall, but it must have been a bore for him. Thank goodness, after the ordeal, I was looked after by two juniors, Keith Hancock and Reggie

Harris, who couldn't have been kinder to a candidate out of his sphere and perhaps slightly sozzled.

Another terror added was the story of a candidate whose ready-made white tie fell into the soup: what then did one do about it? If one had confidence enough one could have ordered it grandly away: 'Bring me another plate of soup – and another white tie.' I recall the embarrassment of our old Anglo-Indian guest, Sir Henry Sharp, when he discovered one evening that he was without his white tie, and couldn't get on with dinner until he went back to his room to fetch it.

Up to the second German war and the levelling of standards in our time the competition for a Prize Fellowship was stiffer, for ours were then almost the only such Fellowships available. Hence, when one reads the Memoirs of the time – memories of such people as Raymond Asquith or John Buchan, John Simon or Halifax – one can see that winning one was considered the blue ribbon of an Oxford career. Since usually only two were elected out of a score or so sitting the examination, it left many disappointed and a trail of envy in Oxford. The College was always the target of some jealousy – very unfairly: it was not its fault, the examination was a fair trial, the elections decided fairly on its result.

Yet I have known Oxford figures who came out well down the list, sixth or seventh, who have continued to resent their non-election – one of them with a kind of vendetta – very unreasonably. If one happened to come out third on the list, two elected ahead of one, one might have some reason to repine, or think that the College had perhaps made a mistake. Not otherwise.

Naturally, the College has sometimes made a mistake and missed some sitting birds. Among those who resented it were Belloc and John Buchan. Belloc was defeated by a much better historian, the medievalist H.W.C. Davis. When Davis's admirable book, *England under the Normans and Angevins*, came out Belloc took the opportunity to attack it in a review. He never had any sense of truth – Trevelyan used to call him, high-mindedly, a 'liar' – and no sense of justice. However, Davis was not a man of genius, Belloc was: I should like to have risked him, and it might have been good for him, if anything could be.

Actually I have heard Birkenhead, the original F.E. Smith, tell the tale of Belloc being dined in College, as usual after the examination. Standing on the hearth-rug in front of the fireplace in the smoking-room, he held forth on the French military manoeuvres. As they left F.E. said to Belloc, 'And do you think you have improved your chances in that ancient house of learning?' Belloc, with masculine imperception, had no idea that he had not.

The College tradition is that he had a heated argument with Hensley Henson about the Dreyfus affair. Belloc, with his usual lack of care for truth, came up with some unknown fact, invented of course, to defeat his opponent. History records how disgracefully the French upper classes, the Army and the Catholic Church behaved in regard to Dreyfus, the shocking anti-Semitism, and how heavily they paid for it. A thousand pities, for one would not want either the Army or the Church, even the upper classes, downgraded, if they had not asked for it.

John Buchan's was a different case. He was defeated by a fellow Scot, an Etonian, trained like a race-horse in the classics, a dab at Latin versification, for what that is worth. Of course he was a better classical scholar than Buchan, though John had already shown his promise by his writing. The moral I draw from this is the immoral one that one should not always go by examination results, at least not solely. One should, if one can, take into account the factor of promise, even relative backgrounds and opportunities, though there we are on chancy ground. Anyhow, I wish the chance had been taken with Buchan, instead of with the race-horse of an Etonian classic.

1. The Twenties

All my life I have been competing against these Etonian and Wykehamist race-horses, and wonder how I have survived. Plodding, I suppose. Sticking at it, as I plodded away for ten or fifteen years at the problems of Shakespeare's biography, the Sonnets, etc – which had defeated everybody – until I had worked out all the answers.

Perhaps the element of some promise *was* taken account of in the case of this working-class boy confronting such competition. I did not write the best essay in the examination, on the uncongenial subject of 'Possessions'. What on earth was one to make of that? I never had had any, so I couldn't put the case for and against. I had hoped for something more literary, and did get my opportunity on other papers, both General and on History, English and European.

Of course I was weak on languages. I had never had the chance, never once been abroad. Maddening, for by nature I was good at languages, definitely at French and rather well read in French literature; Latin poor, for during that war we had been poorly taught in our small Cornish grammar school. When I had been elected, a naughty old professor of military history, who liked it to be thought that he had enjoyed the favours of Sarah Bernhardt, or vice versa, said, 'I notice that your languages are not good. Let me give you a bit of advice: when you go abroad take a dictionary to bed with you.'

This was not at all well received by the young prude I was. Goodness, what an innocent! Also, I was very much of the Left. The rebarbative subject of 'Possessions' – invented by a clever lawyer, Cyril Radcliffe – I had turned into an essay on Property, Aristotle and all that, pro and con. But the College was nothing but tolerant and understanding – put up with all the Leftist nonsense I would not put up with today. They made allowances. And after I went to Germany to learn that uncongenial language, I learned what the

17

facts were, and who had been responsible for the War, the aggression against European civilisation. I had much the same experience, and learned about the Germans, precisely what I found later Maurice Bowra and Kenneth Clark had done.

*

Examining for the Fellowship was a duty that fell mainly upon those of us who resided in College, or in Oxford. The theory was that the whole College examined, and we were assistant-examiners. True, the London element did take part, did scrutinise the papers when they were down at week-ends and expressed their opinions accordingly. We were apt to pay most attention to the essay and the two general papers, from which one could derive an impression of the candidate's general intelligence. Then came the specialist papers – ancient history and philosophy (for Greats candidates); law; medieval and modern history; then, in my time, were added papers in politics, economics, philosophy, for the benefit of candidates from 'Modern Greats'. Some allowance was made for the fact that law candidates were more specialised, and less likely to come up to the standards of others on the general papers. Somewhat easier then to get elected as a lawyer.

Assistant-examiners were properly selected as a mixed bunch to cover these subjects. Naturally rather junior Fellows, closer to the Schools, were to the fore, with a more experienced senior as chairman – report then to go to the College as a whole. Discussion, divisions of opinion, differences of judgment, were sometimes acute. It became difficult to make up one's mind, and it grew harder to weigh candidates from different Schools against each other, especially when yet more papers in English Literature were added, to provide for candidates from that School. Often enough as I was called upon, towards the end I came

1. The Twenties

to find examining for the Fellowships a chore, trying to estimate a wider variety in the field. Earlier it must have been easier – and results perhaps more reliable – with only Greats and Law providing the field. One could sympathise with Grant Robertson: 'Of examining, as of other carnal pleasures, I have at length had a satiety.' (It had fallen to him to award C.R. Attlee the disappointment of a Second in the History School.)

Per contra I remember dear old Oman sighing one day, 'I love examining'; by that time we thought him beyond it. We juniors also thought his subject, military history, out of date. How wrong we were! It proved to be the prime subject of our catastrophic age. Oman had already justified himself as an historian with many books, including those on the Art of War in the Middle Ages, and a vast seven-volume History of the Peninsular War. For this he had ready to hand in the Codrington – of which he was librarian – the papers of Sir Charles Vaughan, our diplomatic envoy in Spain at the time.

Our juvenile sights were set on economics and political theory, in accordance with the fashion of the time. Thus I was delighted, on my first experience of examining, to catch a young economist of promise, which he certainly fulfilled. This was Harry Hodson (was he descended from 'Hodson's Horse'? – he had a rather equine appearance). Curtis shortly coralled him for the Round Table, of whose periodical of that name he became editor. He combined a knowledge of practical economics with Empire affairs, writing on both. Becoming a member of the Reforms Commission of the Government of India qualified him to write a standard book on Partition, *The Great Divide: Britain – India – Pakistan*. After a spell as editor of the *Sunday Times* he ended up as Provost of Ditchley, its prime concern Anglo-American relations. A typical (external) All Souls career, we may say.

Gradually, as economics became more popular as an

academic subject, the College came to contribute its complement to it, exerting a pull from other subjects, sometimes with rewarding results. Denis Rickett equipped himself for a distinguished career in the World Bank in Washington. Douglas Jay combined economics with politics, the former qualifying him for a variegated career in journalism and ministerial posts in Labour governments. I have always remembered being impressed by Jay's examination papers, in spite of (rather than because of) their nervous illegibility. Later I was no less impressed by his response, as a man of high principle, to Beaverbrook's attempt to seduce him away from his job as City Editor of the *Daily Herald* to the *Evening Standard*.

This was Beaverbrook's regular ploy. It worked with irresponsible Leftists. As A.J.P. Taylor admitted blithely, 'Of course Max bribed me, as he did everybody else.' Not everybody was seducible, however. It worked with Tom Driberg, Michael Foot, Malcolm Muggeridge. Of course they were professional journalists making their way, but it amused Beaverbrook, with his itch for mischief, to encourage their making trouble for the responsible Labour leaders, Attlee and Bevin. Even I had an approach from Beaverbrook's right-hand man, G.M. Thomson, to become chief reviewer syndicated throughout their press. I did not consider it for a moment.

A.J. Brown was an economist *pur et simple*, but I respected his practical approach, for economics is a practical subject, not an exercise in mathematical abstractions. Though he became a professor he went on to widespreading practical experience and we saw little of him in College. I was sorry to lose Ian Bowen from history to economics. Later on we recruited as Professor the impeccable John Hicks, whom Roger Makins and I had defeated years before in the Fellowship examination (as also K.B. McFarlane, W.A. Pantin and other worthies).

How many experiences, discussions, tugs-of-war come to

mind! One such was over the relative merits of Denis Brogan *versus* Penderel Moon. Here was a case in point: Brogan was a modern historian, Moon a Greats man. Though I was not a Greats man I recognised the primacy of the Greats School and that it produced the men of highest quality. Brogan was a voluminous historical journalist, who covered pages and pages of information whether relevant or not. Moon's work was of higher quality. Richard Pares backed Brogan, against his fellow Wykehamist Moon: I favoured the Greats man, who won. Pity we couldn't have had both, for both went on to distinguished careers – Brogan in academic life and writing, while Moon made an historic career in India. He wrote well too, concluding with a classic, *The British Conquest and Dominion of India*. The differing judgments between Pares and me were symptomatic.

Over a long life it has been interesting to watch how things work out, sometimes clean contrary to expectations. Here was a case in point: Lionel Butler *versus* Michael Howard. Lionel Butler was an historian with a literary inflexion, rather in my line – and he wrote plenty. Howard kept himself in reserve, wrote little, but in my judgment of higher quality. John Sparrow backed Butler, who won. Michael Howard eventually came to us as professor, the finest military historian in the country – in succession to one Gibbs who sat on the chair for fifteen years and did nothing at all (there are such). Strangely enough, Butler wrote nothing, for all his literary promise, but became unexpectedly a notable administrator, Principal of Royal Holloway College, London.

One day Amery, then a Cabinet Minister, came into the smoking-room with a half-a-crown in his hand: 'See what I've earned.' An American lady wanted to see the Hall (not open to the public). Amery, happening to be outside, showed her in, and on departing she kindly tipped him half-a-crown. True, he was exceptionally short, and had a rather banausic appearance.

*

In those years I sometimes regretted that the College was not more literary, as would have suited me: it was so very political, bent on public affairs – and that in time had its effect on me. We might have had Aldous Huxley, another non-election; instead of whom Geoffrey Faber, E.L. Woodward, and Humphry Sumner were elected. Should I have teamed up with Huxley? I doubt it.[1] There was a Balliol cult of Huxley at the time, much to the fore with Cyril Connolly and John Bowle; but I was not a Balliol man, and I did not share it. Nor could I stand up to the tone of the Garsington set, which I rejected, though encouraged by the alarming favour of Lady Ottoline Morrell.

For the non-election of T.S. Eliot I was partly responsible. He was proposed for a research Fellowship by Faber, on the basis of his typescript Elizabethan Essays. As a junior Fellow, known to write poetry and an admirer of Eliot, I was the only person to possess his Poems, and was asked to lend them around. Ingenuous as ever, it never occurred to me that others might hold them against him. However, when a couple of Scottish Presbyterian professors, MacGregor and Adams, encountered the amenities of 'Lune de Miel':

A l'aise entre deux draps, chez deux centaines de punaises,
La sueur aestivale, et une forte odeur de chienne ...

(what Eliot elsewhere calls 'the good old female stench'), those sons of the manse were shocked and voted him down.

---

[1] However, we did elect another member of that remarkable family later, an ancient historian.

1. The Twenties

It was a blow for Faber, who was struggling to get his firm on its feet. Geoffrey may not have realised how much I had been responsible, inadvertently. I don't think Eliot minded, for he did not fancy college life – he liked only London – and a little later we became friends. But it would have been good to have him in College, an attractive counter-balance to all those heavy-weights in politics and public affairs.

As it was, there was only for literary man charming and sensitive A.S. MacDowall, who wrote the best early book on the Art of Thomas Hardy. He was an admirable essayist, but had wretched health from over-work on *The Times*. So we did not see much of him, and he died early. So too had Herbert Trench, minor poet and theatre man, who gave us the bronze ephebe, Neapolitan reproduction, that acts as centrepiece in our little Common Room garden – and into whose inviting hand Richard Pares, when young, would stuff a handkerchief.

G.M. Young, who might have filled a gap, was at this time in a state of suspense, and did not return until the 1930s. He had gone to stay for the week-end with the formidable Mona Wilson, and never got away again. A couple of highbrows, they were too high-minded to marry, and I think that this had been disapproved of by very 'square' Grant Robertson, another true Scotch believer. Their address in the country was no less indicative, 'The Old Oxyard, Great Oare.' I used to call it Great Bore, when John Sparrow would come back from a week-end there, deploring Miss Wilson's masculine pipe-smoking and insistence on remaining with the men over the port.

Young, excellent scholar and good talker, was the most conceited man I have ever known. When a junior civil servant he was taken by Arthur Henderson on his mission to keep Russia in the war. As such he had a meeting with the Tsar, at the end of his tether. When Young put some point to him, whether we might not lose the war, all he could reply was 'Do you think so?'

The clever young scholar of Callimachus filled in time with verses making fun of Henderson's grammar. Uncle Arthur, no fool, knew two to that one, and simply sacked him. Supercilious Young was rather at a loose end, until Mona came to the rescue. There cannot have been much sex in it, leastways on his side. A famous authority on the Victorians, he once spoke with sympathy for the Prince Consort 'grinding out his duty' with the eager Victoria. Books, I fancy, bound together the occupants of the Old Oxyard.

❖

Perhaps these divagations will serve to give an introductory insight into the life of the College, but we must come to the institution itself. When Archbishop Chichele founded it – with the support of Henry VI – he endowed it with a clutch of estates in Middlesex, Edgware, Cricklewood and Hendon, then in the country. To these were added a few more properties in Oxfordshire, Berkshire, Warwickshire. I remember the names of some of them coming up at College quarterly meetings, repairs and outlays on buildings and drainage, raising or defalcations on rents etc: Lewknor at the foot of the Chilterns, Maids' Moreton with its beautiful church, Marston Trussell farther afield. Whitsundoles regularly came up for a dole at our Whitsun meeting.

One of the estates I was early taken to visit by E.L. Woodward, domestic bursar and fellow historian. This was Padbury in Buckinghamshire. We took with us one of the remarkable series of our estate-maps, made in Elizabethan times for Warden Hovenden, used in ours by R.H. Tawney for the book which founded his reputation as an economic historian. Tyro as I was in these matters, it was fun going over the rumpled ground of the village, tracing the balks and furrows that marked the holdings of peasant farmers long dead – we could even trace their names on the map.

1. The Twenties

In the church it surprised me to find the monument of a Graves–Sawle baronet, of the family that owned the Cornish village of Tregonissey where I was born. What was he doing here? – hunting, I think. Warden Pember had given a little lecture to us newly elected Fellows, Roger Makins and me, on the responsibilities we had as landowners. The dear man mitigated this impressive talk by entering me in the College Register as born in the 'Duchy' of Cornwall – with kind, but inaccurate, intention. (The Duchy is by no means the same thing as the County.)

Though in time I was placed on the estates committee, I never familiarised myself with its business, which became ever more complicated. In earlier centuries All Souls had never been a rich college, unlike Christ Church or Magdalen. And in the agricultural depression of the late 1870s and 1880s Oxford colleges, like all landowners, were badly hit. Warden Anson, a baronet, whose North Country estate profited from urban development, was rumoured to have paid some of the Prize Fellowships out of his own pocket – some £200 a year, in my time £300.

No very exorbitant remuneration, but in addition we had our rooms free, with their exiguous amenities in those days, and opulent dinners in Hall. Cyril Radcliffe described it as 'private squalor, public grandeur'. Indeed when Keynes came over from the luxury of King's, Cambridge, he complained of our spartan bedrooms. He was quite right: they were arctic in winter.

In those gentlemanly days it would never have occurred to us to get up in a College meeting and ask for an increase of salary – very unlike the younger generation after the second German war. I at once set to, and added to my income by teaching, taking pupils from other colleges, examining, writing and reviewing. When that great little man Penderel Moon (not unlike Warden Anson) ceased to be Estates Bursar, he left a note for his successor: 'They are all scroungers.' In their defence it may be said that, since they had incurred the delights of family life, they needed it. But then, they could have added to their income as I did. Shortly my income from other sources far exceeded that from the College, and so it always remained – my All Souls income altogether smaller than my literary earnings. However, traditional College life was geared to a bachelor existence. Warden Anson, model for the generation after him, was a bachelor. He had lived in style: a coach in the stables at the head of the back-drive, liveried footmen in his colours, canary yellow and blue. (I knew the last of them as a College scout, one Tonge.)

In the depth of the agricultural depression Warden Anson took a far-seeing resolution. London was expanding outwards to Edgware, Cricklewood, Hendon. Persuaded by a devoted land-agent, the College raised building loans to develop these estates – and in time All Souls became rich. If one goes to Cricklewood one sees the evidence in the College names recorded in roads, avenues, crescents. I can just remember that agent to whom we owed so much, bearded, brisk, bird-like, little Mr Done. Occasionally he came down to us from his London office, treating the Fellows, his employers, with old-fashioned deference. A very junior Fellow – I had won the Prize at twenty-one – I treated this College servant, to whom we owed so much, if not with deference, at least with marked respect.

Henceforth, then, the estates fell into two groups, with sub-agents, and a Fellow as estates bursar, Geoffrey Faber, responsible to the College. The urban estates brought in increasing returns; the country estates produced a minor proportion of revenue, and some farms made losses which had to be recouped. I never pretended to understand the ins-and-outs of all this; but Leftist as I was politically, I always took a conservative line, was against selling land and in favour of using our surpluses to purchase more. That paid in the end, and was safer anyway. Some colleges prejudiced their long-term future by selling historic properties for immediate financial gain. Though I had no business head, this was not my option.

It turned out that the reward for Warden Anson's far-sightedness was best to be seen in the distinction of the institution in the generation after his death, under Warden Pember. Anson had been elected Warden as a reformer in 1871, and remained at his post till he died in 1914. He was regarded with veneration as almost a second Founder, which he was. His monument in Chapel, with his effigy, occupies the position of a Founder, on the left hand of the altar. The monument of Archbishop Chichele in Canterbury cathedral we keep in repair and repaint from time to time.

Anson was a Balliol man, an early pupil of Jowett, as Warden Pember and R.W. Lee were later. (Lee told me that Jowett was by no means the caricature that people made of him; in fact a sharp customer, a greatish man.) Anson was imbued with Jowett's ideas of preparing men for service to the state, picking them carefully with his keen eye. Jowett had dressed down the young Cosmo Lang, telling him that it was not his business to reform the East End of London but to get a First in the School of Literae Humaniores. Lang went on with his reforming – and got a Second in the Schools. He had to go on to a First in History and a second attempt at All Souls before he was elected. This had its consequences.

For one thing, in the rivalry with Henson. Hensley Henson had been elected before him – and uniquely, not from a college, but as a 'tosher', a Non-Collegiate student. Lang had had all the advantages – and spent them on good works. In the course of electing Fellows a Common Room meeting is held at which evidence is given as to the personal qualities of candidates. On this occasion Henson ended up his speech: 'In short, Mr Warden, Mr Lang is a man of second-rate ability and first-rate gifts.'

Lang certainly had first-rate gifts – not for nothing was

he a cousin of Matheson Lang, the actor. But he was not a popular figure in College, as Henson was. People are always envious of grandees, and Lang was, very properly, grand: he had his dignity to maintain, an archbishop before forty, 'the youngest Archbishop of York since Paulinus'. Henson could not forgive his junior for getting so far ahead of him up the episcopal ladder. He was a natural wit, which Lang was not. One day at Bishopthorpe, the Archbishop was showing him the unfriendly portrait Orpen had painted of him – 'People say that it makes me look proud, pompous and prelatical.' Henson took his opportunity: 'And to which of these epithets does your Grace object?'

Lang was never unpopular with me, from the first moment. On the first night one dines as a Fellow one's health is drunk in champagne. I was sitting beside the Archbishop, who noticed that I hesitated; I was a water-drinker – had never met champagne. Lang at once put me at ease, and rather grandly: 'I am a water-drinker too, but on these occasions I give myself a dispensation.' Nobody could have appreciated the liturgical note more than I, and thus dispensed I took a sip of the disagreeable fizz.

Lang was always kind to young men, and would sometimes tell me things. About his relations with Queen Victoria, who wondered why he did not marry; or George V, who could not bear missionary sermons, or sermons longer than twenty minutes at most. The Archbishop became a friend and confidant of the King, who must have told him all his worries about his son and heir. While Archbishop of York Lang remained a Fellow, and came to College for week-ends after a week's work in London. When he succeeded to Canterbury he became our official Visitor, and could come only rarely as such.

After his retirement he returned, and could now let his hair down (by this time he hadn't any left). After one of Henson's pin-pricks I dared to say to Lang, how could he expect an ultimate position of responsibility – and say whatever he liked? 'Precisely,' said Lang, who had absolute control over himself, Henson not. The latter had fancied himself for York. I heard Henson preaching in Chapel, looking across at Lang in his stall, hiss through ill-fitting dentures, 'My predecessor, the great Bishop Butler, declined the primacy because he would not be a pillar of a declining Church.' Lang gave no sign that he even heard: he must have had to put up with too much nonsense from pulpits in his time even to listen.

Henson was indeed a very different cup of tea, and my first encounter with him was characteristic too. He must have been told that I was a working-class Leftist. So the vibrant little figure in purple said, 'Isn't it time for a little blood-letting of the working-classes?' I caught his eye. We both laughed, and from that moment became friends. He was warm-hearted, but that sort of *boutade* was precisely what got him into trouble with people who had no sense of humour.

He might have been content with the palatine see of Durham, where he lived in Auckland Castle on the edge of the coal-field, 'like a whale stranded on the sea-coast of Patagonia'. ('Minnow' would have been more appropriate.) He one day said in the hearing of historian Woodward that, if this were the Middle Ages his wife would be a Princess Palatine. Woodward, who had no good blood for bishops, knew better: she would not have been a Princess Palatine, but a concubine.

Woodward was not a generous man, he had earlier fancied himself as a cleric, and enjoyed a Pusey House period wearing a biretta. Richard Pares and I, who jibbed somewhat under his disapprobation of the younger generation as domestic bursar – as such he was a bit pompous – did not let him forget his ecclesiastical aberration, and always called him the Abbé. I liked him well enough when he was boyish and off his high horse. But he thought me uppish, and took it upon him to put me down. He was the only one who did, and constantly. This was not good for a young fellow already wrought up with duodenal trouble from years of strain and anxiety, and it was, by a Celt, resented.

Only one other Fellow I had not much liking for: this was the venerable chaplain, Arthur Johnson, a hunting type. He had had the ill luck to get married young, and so lost his Fellowship. He and his wife had to work very hard at tutoring, examining, lecturing to make a living. In my first term he took me for a walk around Magdalen to see his Siberian ducks. Along Addison's Walk he tried to bully me as to whether or not I would have fought in the late war. I had been brought up under the Leftist nonsense of Brailsford, Bertrand Russell and Co that we were as responsible for the 1914-18 war as the Germans. Of course I was wrong, but I wasn't going to argue the toss with this old boy, or be bullied by him. I remained mute, to his annoyance, and took no notice of his Siberian ducks.

He was an irritable type; so was I – privately to myself I used to describe him as *hargneux*. Our next encounter was in the Acland Home – with which I became very familiar. I had had a narrow escape from a perforated ulcer and peritonitis. I was reading Renan's *Vie de Jésus* when Johnson came to see me. He was not very welcome, until he said, 'I suppose you never saw Renan?' Of course I hadn't; but I was fascinated by Renan as a fellow Celt and read all I could of him. Johnson had heard him when he came to lecture at Oxford, but, like a person of no imagination, was neither impressed by nor enlightening about him.

One thing I had in common with Henson, if not more: we not only loved the College, but regarded it as home. He had had a most uncongenial home life, with a fanatical Nonconformist father who, though he could have afforded it, would not send his clever boy to a Public School, for fear of his morals. He would not even let him go to a university

30

until persuaded by Henson's stepmother, and then only on condition that he did not enter a college. The result was that Henson always regretted that he had not been through the proper classical course of his contemporaries. He emerged, like me, none the worse for it, an historian.

When he came into the bosom of All Souls he felt that this was his proper home. He tells us that he loved everybody from the Warden to the pantry boy. (Lang could never have committed himself to that dubious proposition.) Henson regarded Warden Anson as a father, and he became an *enfant terrible* of the society. People still remembered his sayings and doings when I came into it. He was so diminutive that he could mount the mantelpiece in the Common Room, the bust of Wren looking down on him, to address the table below. To Oman, arriving late in Chapel – he was always hurrying in late: 'You arrive late, not only for the General Confession but for the Absolution you most stand in need of.' At Sidmouth, where he stayed for the vacation – he was a West Countryman – an organ-grinder played outside his lodgings during the fortnight: 'It combined the *ennui* of eternity with the torments of the damned.' On the cold mutton for lunch in buttery: 'I accepted it without enthusiasm; I reject it with alacrity.' No wonder his notorious phrase about the 'Protestant underworld' largely helped to sink the new Prayer Book in Parliament. He was indeed a liability on the bench of bishops, a headache for Archbishop Lang, but always fun.

He twice invited me to Auckland Castle; alas, I never went, until after his death. Lang never invited anybody, except ecclesiastics. He had a burdened life of it, and once described it as 'unbearable, intolerable, inevitable'. I understood, with sympathy, these two remarkable, complex men. It is more difficult to understand simpletons, there is so little to make out. Lang was always accused of being a snob – he knew two to that one. I had no difficulty

31

in defending him, in the *New Statesman*: 'He found interesting people more interesting than uninteresting ones.'

More seriously, I found something touching about both men. They had found their vocation, made their profession – in the religious sense – when the Church was still a foremost part of the national life. They were left high and dry at the end of their lives, by the movement of the time. Henson had dedicated himself to Christ, alone in Iffley church, laying his hand on the altar. Lang had undergone a conversion. Coming away from Cuddesdon church at Easter time, and returning across Shotover, he heard a voice calling him into the Church. It is a vanished world.

Of the College bishops Headlam was again a very different character. Dermot Morrah said of him, he was neither High Church, nor Low Church, nor Broad Church – but Hard Church. He was a North Countryman, a country gentleman with a Durham estate: one of the Victorian clergy who put into the Church more than they got out of it. On the other hand, of his palace at Gloucester: 'I like a *large* house.' He was never better off than when Principal of King's College, London, with a house and £1,200 a year. And what a hard life a bishop's was: a fourteen-hour day, and of the day's dozen or fifteen letters a couple would be not only offensive but obscene.

There was a soft side to this hard carapace. Much later, during the Second War, Headlam shared my inner green room with me, and I shared with him my extra ration of milk as a duodenal subject. The old countryman loved flowers: the wild flowers that flourished in Victorian days right up to the towns had all been devastated by the indiscriminate picking of our time – the filthy population explosion again!

One day G.M. Trevelyan's daughter was my guest. Suddenly the door behind her opened, and out popped this large, gorilla-like figure, face twitching with nervous grimaces. A shock for her. Headlam was a descendant of Oliver Cromwell and, it was said, of Peter the Great. One can't be certain about the latter, but he looked as if he might be. In younger years his fortune had been told by a gypsy, who detected in his large cricketer's hands his stormy passions. 'But well under control,' he said. Hence the nervous twitches and grimaces.

He would tell me things too, that went back to the Victorian age, gave me a sense of being in touch with it. Here was a valuable function the senior Fellows performed for one as a junior, whether they knew it or not – I appreciated it, loved them for it, and profited greatly from it. One night Frederick Temple when Bishop of London was driven back late from the House of Lords to Fulham Palace. Temple was a bit mean, and gave the cabby an inadequate tip. This Victorian worthy protested. Would St Paul have given him that? No, said the Bishop of London, but you would have been driving him not to Fulham but to Lambeth. An unthinkable exchange today.

The hard features were uppermost. Our bishop invited a junior Fellow to accompany him on a confirmation tour 'to see what fools my clergy are'. He was not far out. Up in the Cotswolds one dotty parson had alienated his parish and emptied his church. Headlam took the trouble to visit and get them all back again. Next Sunday the parson got out of his pulpit, went outside the church, locked the congregation in and grinned in through the windows at them. A good joke; but who'd be a bishop? Headlam confided to me whether it would not have been better to remain a professor and finish his theological work. One day in the coffee-room, to which we resorted for private converse, I happened to hear Headlam and Lang deploring the antics of the absurd Winnington-Ingram, then Bishop of London.

Of other College clerics two were Headmasters of the two first schools in England, Cyril Alington of Eton, A.T.P. Williams of Winchester. Both were so hard at work that we saw little of them. Williams was an unobtrusive, uncommunicative man. Richard Pares told me that his sermons would begin, 'As we turn over the pages of history' – and there would follow an admirable history lecture. He had a stiff argument with the rationalist young Penderel Moon to get him to consent to being confirmed. In the end it came to there being no case for being an exception.

Alington, a handsome man who had all the gifts, was a splendid Headmaster of Eton – he held the boys in thrall with his Fables told in Chapel. He had made a dynastic marriage with a Lyttelton (with whom G.M. Trevelyan had been in love). Alington was so successful that, like Lang, he was the target of much envy – unavoidable, people being what they are. Again, he was nothing but kind to this *enragé* young Leftist and asked me several times over to Eton. I would never go – inferiority-complex held me back. After his time I did go, to lecture to their Literary Society (headed by young Waldegrave) on the Problems of Shakespeare's Sonnets. They formed the most intelligent audience on that subject I have ever encountered, in England or America.

Of the chaplains Johnson's one qualification was the silvery voice with which he read the services in Chapel. They were very old-fashioned Regency Use, northward position at the altar; our prayer-books prayed for the Dowager Queen Adelaide. Headlam, as a reformer, tried to get a theological Fellow elected to prepare for Johnson's retirement. At that the old man rose: 'In the course of a long life I have learned three things: never ask for anything, never refuse anything, and never resign anything.' That finished Headlam.

As Bishop of Gloucester he also wanted to lever out our Senior Fellow, Cholmondeley, from the family living of Adlestrop, which he had held for half a century. He harked back to Founder's Kin, of whom he was one – an aristocratic innocent, a bleating old sheep. (However, he

34

had won the Newdigate – I only a *proxime* – and knew Edward Thomas's poem, 'Adlestrop'.) The characteristics of these clerics were summed up briefly by Henson accordingly: 'the militant churchmanship of Cholmondeley, the mellow charm of Headlam, and the pastoral simplicity of the Archbishop of York.' Lang was indeed a curial figure, would have made a perfect cardinal.

In the private fantasy life I lived there in early days I wished that the excellent acoustics of the Chapel might be taken advantage of for a Byrd or Palestrina Mass. No such hope in that unmusical society – we *said* the prayers and responses to each other prosaically, Grant Robertson gabbling ahead, with alternate verses of the Psalms. Sometimes when there alone I would try out the plainsong, 'Credo in unum deum, patrem omnipotentem, factorem terrae et caeli.'

A happier successor to Johnson was F.E. Hutchinson, a spare figure with an ingratiating manner, like a clergyman out of Trollope. This did not appeal to John Sparrow, who represented Pember's tradition of Rationalist secularism. But I respected Hutchinson and was fond of him. At a BBC committee the little man stood up to the towering Director Reith – a 'Wuthering Height' as Churchill called him – and dressed him down. Reith was so taken aback that he gave way. Hutchinson was not proud of his exploit, it was just that his conscience was aroused. He was a good scholar of seventeenth-century literature, descended from the Puritan Colonel and Lucy Hutchinson. So later I got him to write the Milton volume in the series *Men and their Times*, which I was to edit.

V.J.K. Brook was an outsider, an administrator, a Censor of the Non-Collegiate Students. Not an intellectual, he surprised me by a first-class sermon – and we constituted a difficult audience to please. Since he was Low Church I used to tease him with what a fine pair of shoulders he had which called for a cope. He was rather teasable, but was a man of strong common sense. He came back one day from a sermon preached by C.S. Lewis at the peak of his war-time *réclame*, to a crowded congregation. This was on the Resurrection. Lewis had insisted – with his usual combination of credulity and dogmatism – on belief in every circumstance of it, 'nails and all'. Our chaplain was affronted by Lewis's nonsense. However, as Charles II said of leaders of political parties, I dare say 'his nonsense suited their nonsense'.

When John McManners came to preach to us I was moved to tears by what he said. Not so Warden Sparrow: no imagination, quite unmoved. The College was lucky to recruit McManners for chaplain – two heroic sons in the Falklands operations – but that was after my time.

It is curious that I should have concentrated so much on the clerics, who were after all a small minority. Perhaps that reveals an unconscious affinity. But I must turn to the seculars.

CHAPTER 2

Warden Pember

Warden Pember was indeed a secular figure, I don't think he had any religious belief at all, a Whig Rationalist. He was not a man of ideas of his own, his whole idea was to keep the College going on the lines laid down by Anson, and that was a good line. He reaped the reward of presiding over a distinguished company whom Anson had picked and who fulfilled his hopes by occupying some of the first positions in the nation's life, in the Empire as well as in Church and State. Not that Pember was an Empire man, he didn't care for the group inspired by Rhodes and Milner, the 'Kindergarten'. A Balliol friend of Grey and Asquith, he was a Little Englander.

Immensely distinguished himself in appearance, a handsome Harrovian, he was a first-class classic, given to Latin versification, and a worthy cricketer. He had had a formidable father, also a lawyer and classic, and was conscious of not being up to his father's shoes. This was, as usual, a depressive influence. His wife was no less formidable – 'Frank has to be taken up to every one of his fences.' His only son had been killed early in the war, and this – as with dear Quiller Couch – unnerved him. Such a tragedy did not unnerve the still more vulnerable Kipling, it nerved him to a hatred for the Germans, who were responsible.

Pember hated no one; he was a cool man, somewhat negative; but he was more than kind to me. Come to think of it – I did not realise it at the time – his attitude to me was rather paternal. He kept an eye on me at College meetings, in Hall, in Common Room, an appealing, appreciating eye, and noticeably invited me along to lunch at the Lodgings when he had literary folk to entertain, like the Buchans, down from Elsfield. He was an excellent host; such old-fashioned Victorian courtesy. A constant reader, he wrote nothing, but was a good *raconteur*.

I was early on present at an exchange before the smoking-room fire between Oman and the Warden. Oman said: 'I wonder how many Fellows there are who have never written a book at all.' He had written many, and was not partial to Pember, who replied: 'Not many, even if only a book of Statutes.' And he gave me a knowing look, almost a wink. I hadn't much sense, but the exchange was not lost on me. The Warden had been a member of the Statutory body that had followed upon the post-war University Commission. There he had been in place to safeguard the position of All Souls, and – rather naughtily, I thought – to dump the chair of Empire history away from the College upon Balliol. (Though a Leftist, I was, like Ernest Bevin, all in favour of the British Empire: weren't Africans and Indians happier, prevented from massacring each other, in those better days?) Reggie Coupland made a first-class historian of the Empire: the only disapprobation the Warden would express was to mispronounce his name Cowpland.

In place of the Beit Chair of Colonial History Pember accepted that of French Literature, which had nothing to do with our main subjects of interest. I thought that it ought to have gone to Queen's, already invested in Modern Languages. Gustave Rudler, the Professor, was a dull man, though the leading authority on the far from dull subject of Benjamin Constant and Madame de Stael. Madame Rudler was what Lady Firth called a 'honey-pot'. They did their duty in bringing over literary figures to lecture, and included me, though very junior, in their entertainments – they knew my interest in French literature.

Thus I met poets, like Fernand Gregh and Pierre Jean Jouve, who were but names to me from the *Nouvelle Revue Française*, which I took regularly.[1] Madame Halévy was a more striking figure than her husband, the historian Elie Halévy, who wrote the famous *History of the English People in the Nineteenth Century*. He had been struck, one learned, by the importance of Methodism and the religious sects early in the century: that inspired him.

The most memorable figure was Paul Valéry, whom I met on two occasions. On the later occasion, since I was well up in his aesthetics, I asked, rather pointedly, if there would be a 'politique de Valéry'. This got an electric response: Never, 'je suis *épouvanté*!' Well, weren't we all, as the Thirties wore on?

Pember was not Anson's choice to succeed him. This was really Grant Robertson, a leading figure in College, a star lecturer in the History School, an academic *pur sang*. The younger Conservative element had favoured Foster Cunliffe, a Yorkshire baronet who was estates bursar. This fine upstanding fellow was killed in the first German war. At the Election to succeed Anson in 1914 John Simon ran Grant Robertson too hard on Party lines – they were both devout Radicals. Pember may have emerged as a compromise candidate, the subject of Oman's only unkind remark: a 'Returned Empty', i.e. from London, where Pember had not made a great mark at the Parliamentary Bar.

However, he was well qualified to make an agreeable Warden; he was independently well off, equipped with a wife, also well off, to entertain at the Lodgings. She was the daughter of Lord Justice Davey, victim of one of young F.E.

---

[1] After the second War, which cut us off so sadly from France, I gave my file of back-numbers to the French Institute.

Smith's well-known insolences. The elderly judge happened to spit out his false teeth in court, whereupon F.E. inquired blandly, 'Something fell from your lordship?' I don't think that the Hon. Mrs Pember had much use for junior Fellows, nor they for her; she was not popular, the Warden was, for he was a dear man. She cared more for gardening at Broncroft Castle in Shropshire, where they were neighbours of Stanley Baldwin, another Harrovian classic. I have observed the Warden, self-conscious as ever, walking down the length of the Codrington with his old friend, then Prime Minister, a less handsome, indeed homely, but more assured figure.

I suspect that, on merit, Grant Robertson should have been elected: a more positive figure, with a policy – though that might have had its disadvantages and divided the College. He immediately hived off to Birmingham, where he made a first-class Vice-Chancellor. As Napoleon said of himself, he had 'le goût de la fondation', and had two historic achievements to his credit. He started the well-known Medical School there, and got going the Barber Institute of Art, with its splendid collection of pictures. Kindness itself to me – practically all those senior Fellows were as kind as they were gentlemen – he took me over to see the collection before even the gallery was open. Introduced to the celebrated director, Thomas Bodkin, I opened up with enthusiasm for a lovely picture by a not well-known Pre-Raphaelite I had just seen at Sheffield. (I remember it fifty-sixty years after – was it by Collinson?) It turned out that Bodkin was *the* authority on the painter and – an Irish type – thought I was flattering him. Nothing of the sort, it was ingenuous enthusiasm – though there might have been a psychic element between two Celts.

Grant Robertson would have made a more active Warden. Warden Pember had no sense of time; College meetings went on and on. Lang, who had an acute sense of time as of everything else, left his grandfather-clock to the

Common Room, with special intention – he could not bear sitting on and on over the port. Robertson was rather a teetotaller, also a religious believer. It is said that he prevented the election of Graham Wallas as Professor of Political Theory, on the ground that he did not believe in divine Revelation. So a fellow Scotch believer was elected, W.G.S. Adams: not in the same class as Wallas as a thinker, and he wrote nothing. Oman described Adams's field as 'the Wider Oneness'.

Warden Pember attended upon all his duties religiously, even reading our books (what *can* he have thought of my *Politics and the Younger Generation*!), if in no religious spirit. Dick Crossman wrote of Warden Fisher of New College, another Whig Rationalist, attending Chapel, 'like an up-ended sarcophagus', as if not wholly present. At time of College meetings, quarterly, there was a Communion service, College officials dutifully communicating. The unbelieving element, led by bearded Spenser Wilkinson in spats, withdrew at the ante-Communion, and I dared to follow suit. It was an awkward walk out. Cyril Radcliffe called it 'the most difficult walk in life', as one passed the Warden – those features, not exactly chiselled, but noble, did not perhaps blench, but one might say flinched, as I caught his eye and passed on down those slippery marble steps and out into the open air.

What then was one doing in Chapel? I used to scan the stained-glass windows, and watch the flickering lights and shadows, hear the bells of other colleges and churches ringing across the roofs of Oxford. It made a beautiful intermission, a suspension of time; I turned my thoughts to the past, or contemplated the countenances of the assembled Fellows. When we turned to the east for the Creed, there was the great stone screen to contemplate, with all these figures of the remote past, of the Hundred Years War.

Actually, the figures were Victorian reconstructions, and

some of the Fellows were recognisable – Lord Salisbury, the Prime Minister, for one, and Lord Bathurst, who had paid for it, for another. Had it been a good idea, I wondered, to undo the Georgian classicism and re-Gothicise the interior? The Victorians had the courage of their convictions; so had the Georgians. These last, in the days of the poet Young, had paid a large sum for the leading painter in Rome at the time, Raphael Mengs, to paint us a grand picture of the Magdalen, a *Noli me tangere* to place over the altar, classical surround, panelling and all. This was swept away, but not Thornhill's grandiose screen at the entrance, which went with it.

When I came into College there were still daily services, morning and evening. Short as they were, I found it rather a chore to turn out for Chapel at 8 a.m., before breakfast. Even at Christ Church that had not been demanded of undergraduates. Shortly this came to an end for want of attendance; services were concentrated un-liturgically at week-ends, and I attended irregularly, as the mood and convenience fell.

Our Chapel services were very prosaic; we read the verses of the Psalms for the day to each other, alternating with the chaplain. Once, in the smoking-room, I witnessed old Johnson ticking a Cabinet Minister off. This was Leo Amery, who was remarking to me that the constitution of the British Empire was inexplicable, like the Trinity. Johnson, overhearing this, intervened angrily. Amery should not use such a comparison, such unsuitable language. 'The Holy Trinity was a Holy Mystery.' I was surprised by how well Amery took this. He said nothing, but smiled broadly to me as the old boy left.

Johnson had been a leader among the college tutors who ostracised Sir Charles Firth, after his Inaugural Lecture as Regius Professor advancing the claims of historical research before those of teaching.

I had no need of Johnson's ministrations. But he was

called in aid of that invaluable commodity, Morrah's immortal soul, when wavering on the brink of going over to Rome. In vain, of course. A singularly unpersuasive cleric.

✤

A subsidiary category of Fellows were professors; it was an old humour of the grandees to regard them as helots. The joke was not completely apposite, for some of these worthies had been originally Prize Fellows, i.e. real All Souls timber, and the College had endowed some of these professorships, i.e. Chichele chairs. The grandee attitude to professoring was best expressed by a Cambridge man, Maynard Keynes: 'I will not have the indignity of the title without the advantage of the emolument.' The most famous economist there, he was never a professor of economics. Today there are too many of them, with their conflicting nostrums: it is a *practical* subject, to be learned in practice, applied in action; no point in it as a kind of abstract geometry.

Yet this is what it was to our Professor of Economic Theory, F.Y. Edgeworth, the prime mathematical economist in the country. Roy Harrod had a cult of him, though what his contribution to the subject was I am unable to say. Few could follow him. I remember the old gentleman perfectly. Half-Irish, of that famous family, half-Spanish, he was of an exquisite courtesy, with a marvellous oblique indirection of speech. Halifax, in his own autobiography, *Fulness of Days*, has a few comic examples of it. Nobody could get a direct opinion out of Edgeworth; he one day admitted that he 'loved the duplicity of things'.

When he discovered that I was at the time stuck on Marxism and the M.C.H. (the Materialist Conception of History), then fashionable on the Left, Edgeworth did come out with the definite opinion that Marx's economics were no good. Neither, I dare say, were his. I was more amused when he told me that his aunt, or great-aunt, famous Maria Edgeworth of Edgeworthstown, would not allow him to say Brighton, he was to say Brighthelmstone. It was impressive when he asked incidentally if I had read Voltaire's *Henriade* – he had. On his one journey to America, sea-sick in his cabin most of the voyage, he occupied his mind reconstructing the *Iliad*, and could do about a half of it.

Unmarried, he lived in College; he had come to the brink of marriage, but he and his intended had disagreed about a carpet. Only recently did I learn that Beatrice Potter rejected his proposal, thinking him ugly – and then married the tadpole Sidney Webb! In my first year I attended several funerals of these bearded old gentlemen. As an undergraduate I had never been inside the walls – though I had read Froude's essay in which it occurred – and thought of it as a kind of *morgue*. It was then a queer place for a lonely young Celt.

In academe there was a fixation, a cult, perhaps a slogan, as to the necessity of research. My chief friend, Richard Pares, a professor's son, was bitten with it. The word had no terrors for Henson, who described it as 'that state of resentful coma dignified by the name of Rezearch'. He pronounced it thus by way of contempt – and went off to do good work in the East End of London, holding one of the two best College livings, that of Barking, while Headlam had Welwyn, Edward Young's old haunt. (Did Henson really address his parishioners as 'Ye Barking Christians'? He told his mate, Pember, that he always wrote his sermons to curb his tendency to loquacity, or, we may think, for fear of what he might say.)

Actually, All Souls had nibbled a bit at the *monstrum horrendum*. It had supported the endless researches of Lord Acton, who, like some others, could not bring himself to the point of writing them up. Gratefully, he wished his enormous library to come to us; but on the plea that it would duplicate the Codrington, we relinquished it to Cambridge, where it made the nucleus of the History Faculty's Library. Next, the voluminous S.R. Gardiner was supported – another descendant of Oliver Cromwell, spiritually too, for he was a Plymouth Brother. He was followed by the Tudor historian A.F. Pollard, not a genial type.

Finally, the College descended – as if to bear out Henson – to an economist, one N.B. Dearle, dullest of men. This provoked the poem of the far from dull Raymond Asquith, which began,

'How unpleasant to walk the Turl
With Spenser Wilkinson [another bore], or Dearle.'

Was this the poem that ended with the simile,

'like a bishop's bottom, ruddy and round and hot.'?

The King Charles's head of Research came to the fore in the discussions as to what we should do with our prosperity, our surplus revenues. Warden Pember would pronounce the word self-consciously, revénues, looking to see how I took it. It never occurred to any of us that we should spend it on ourselves, though shortly junior Fellows had a rise from £200 a year to the princely sum of £300.

The now wealthy College was markedly generous to the university. A large subsidy went annually to the upkeep of the Bodleian Library; a regular fund went to the Non-Collegiate Students, perhaps a polite propitiation for the abolished Bible Clerks; and even to more indigent colleges. I do not suppose that this made us any more loved – certainly not by Maurice Bowra, struggling gallantly to keep Wadham's head above water. (He sold off part of their extensive garden, to build Rhodes House.)

This raised the lugubrious spectre of what College policy

should be. Since the Warden gave no lead, the two Bursars, Faber and Woodward, took the bull by the horns. There was something bullish about Geoffrey Faber; I always got on well with him, but opposition made him go red in the face – he was a high-coloured Rugbeian, back from the war. These two, who ran the College under Pember, recruited him to the idea of spending our money on science, a lot of science Fellows. The Warden was not averse; his daughter was married to Sir Charles Darwin, head of that prodigious family – Pember progeny were all Darwins.

In the seventeenth century there had been a brilliant flowering of science at Oxford, from which the Royal Society took its rise. In this All Souls played its part, with the young Christopher Wren, then mathematician and experimenter; we had his death-mask, which I often contemplated, in the Codrington, and five great folios of his plans and designs for London churches, palaces and houses. I regularly got out the volume devoted to St Paul's to show to visitors. In Hall we had the portrait of Thomas Sydenham, foremost practising physician of that time. The Library had his Latin book on the prevalent venereal disease: he evidently thought that gonorrhea and syphilis were two stages of the same distemper. John Mayow was a physiologist who wrote on respiration, also on rickets. He was a brilliant Cornishman who died young.

This should have made me sympathetic to re-colonising science with us; but I had other ideas. Science was being increasingly provided for by the university, and some other colleges; once admitted it absorbed all available funds, like caterpillars eating up the cabbage leaf. The dominant subjects of the College were history and law; we had already branched out naturally into politics and economics, founding a chair in Political Theory and Institutions, held by W.G.S. Adams, and another in Political Economy, held by D.H. MacGregor, a Cambridge man, Edgeworth's successor. The way forward to my mind, in keeping with the nature of the College, was not in natural science but the social sciences.

The university had just successfully launched the new School of PPE – Philosophy, Politics and Economics – called Modern Greats for short. We should aim at taking a lead in that. I had it in mind that we should make our Readership in Economic History into a full professorship. We should go on to create a chair in Social (not Physical) Anthropology. The latter inflexion had received a rude shock with the scandal of the bogus finds at Glozel, which ruined the reputation of Solomon Reinach – shortly to be followed by the similar scandal of Piltdown Man. Headlam on Glozel: 'If this is what anthropologists think we theologians can think what we like.' No investment in dubious subjects – stick to the social sciences.

To clear the way for those more promising developments it was necessary to defeat the Bursars' project. As a matter of tactics the College was divisible into three parts: one third supported Faber and Woodward's science proposals; one third, conservatives like Oman, wanted no new move; and my junior group, faithfully supported by Richard Pares and G.F. Hudson ('Chinese Hudson' John Betjeman called him). Unite those last two-thirds, and we would have a majority. In the decisive debate at College meeting Pares was amused to see me go out to fetch Oman, shepherding him in to vote the right way.

We had a majority: the way was clear for my positive proposals, and the documents show that one by one they were acted upon. Our first Professor of Social Anthropology was a Cambridge man, A.R. Radcliffe-Brown: we were less impressed by him than he was. For the chair of Economic History G.N. Clark, a former Prize Fellow, was elected. I dare say the Reader in the subject, E. Lipson, should have had it: he had been Reader for years and made the subject his own. Clark was a very clever man, who promised something new. J.H. Clapham from Cambridge, *doyen* of the subject and an elector, told me that my article in the *Criterion* on Clark's historical work had been cited in his favour. G.N. became a close, though cool, friend. He wanted to recruit me as a colleague at Oriel, but I did not want to be a college tutor.

The inflexion of All Souls was reinforcing my *engouement* with politics. Whether this was fortunate or unfortunate I cannot say, and anyway I cannot blame the College atmosphere for turning my sights that way. It was reinforced when Sir Arthur Salter succeeded Adams as Professor of Political Theory and Institutions. He had had a distinguished career as a civil servant in Whitehall and Geneva, and was incapable of going back to the grind of Aristotle-Hobbes-Locke-Rousseau. So I was appointed Lecturer to fill in for him, and it turned out that these lectures in political theory were all the lecturing I did for the university. This again reinforced my interest in politics. But this is to anticipate.

I had by then already done a good deal of tutoring in political theory as well as history. Junior Fellows were allowed to take pupils from other colleges, up to a maximum of twelve hours a week, the rest of the time for our own work. I taught up to the maximum, and tutors make better teachers when young and fresh from the Schools – and I had no lack of pupils, whom I taught conscientiously, if somewhat aggressively. Also rather effectively – one of them got a First, who should never have done so. Then shot himself.

Two of my earliest pupils were from Lady Margaret Hall. The women came *à deux*, to chaperone each other, and my two girls were not much younger than I was. Veronica Wedgwood was accompanied by a pretty piece, an orphan who was a small heiress, with a rich sexy voice and an attractively hesitant stutter. She was not hesitant in other ways: the young tutor was fair game, and she attracted attention away from clever Veronica, who sat back and allowed her to take the floor. Once, on the excuse that she was going out to dinner, she came arrayed in a marvellous silk dress in all the colours of the rainbow. Making her mark in Schools was not her aim. She did not succeed in distracting me as much as, perhaps, she thought. All the same, when she announced to me, in the garden at Wadham, that she was getting engaged to someone else, I did feel a little the pang of jealousy she intended.

Anyway, I couldn't get engaged to anybody; and anyhow, like Arthur Balfour when asked why he hadn't married Margot Asquith, 'I rather fancied a career for myself'. Periodically I was tormented by that early-formed duodenal ulcer, though I didn't know what it was that winged me. When I was elected the doubt had been expressed whether I would stay in College, or whether I would take off for London, like other birds. In the event increasing ill-health, with increasing ulceration, decided for me. Fortunately, Shakespeare says that a bad blow to one often turns out for good. This was my case all the way along. Life in politics would have killed me in short time. Again, if I had had normal health, I had so much mental energy and such obstinacy that I should have killed myself that way. Already I was over-working.

I don't wish to be sentimental, but for years I had been under strain and worry. 'De l'audace et toujours de l'audace', or Disraeli's 'sanitas sanitatum, omnia sanitas' – I might have said, 'Examination after examination, nothing but examinations.' *One* university scholarship for the whole of Cornwall – I *had* to get it or fall by the wayside. What would have happened to me if I hadn't won the scholarship in English Literature at Christ Church? How proud I was to be a Scholar of the House, and to have been chosen by a man of genius, J.D. Beazley, friend of Flecker. Now *winged*! I was very resentful, always anxious to do my best, and now caught, trapped ...

My trouble reached a crisis with the ulcer perforating

and peritonitis. Here too was a moral. My charming young doctor never read the symptoms. It took a clever Fellow of All Souls, Reggie Harris, to read the 'Hippocratic look' on my face – I was slipping easily out of life – and see the urgency of an operation. Is it any wonder that I *hate* stupidity? My doctor, a nice man who became a friend, apologised to me after I had nearly slipped through the net, and said that in his training he had never encountered duodenal ulcer. Good God, after my long experience, I could treat anyone afflicted with it.

It was a periodic trouble; in the intervals I enjoyed life and worked harder than ever, plus a great deal of teaching, beginning with pupils from my old college. Evidently successfully, for I was asked by my former tutor to stand for the well-paid tutorial Studentship (i.e. Fellowship) advertised there. Without thinking much about it, I assumed that my old College knew best and would look after me. After subjecting me to the humiliation of an interview, when they all knew me well enough, they appointed somebody else, senior to me, from another college, with a superior background. They were entirely within their rights, and in my opinion were quite right to do so.

But I never forgave the superfluous humiliation, for I had not really wanted the job or to be a life-long teaching hack. At the interview Robin Dundas, who was one, put a baited question which settled my hash. 'Would you be more interested in teaching the more intelligent pupils, or the less intelligent?' Ingenuously I answered, 'The more intelligent.' This was not in line with the average run of Christ Church men. I had never met with rejection, or been defeated before, and this humiliation by my old College was a bitter blow – I had been *asked* to stand.

The humiliation was never forgiven. But, worse, it started a fierce rejection-complex which came up at other junctures whenever I depended on other human beings – I never failed when depending on myself. I recognised the roots of this complex, in part. Less sensitive and more normal, conventional types could take set-backs from others more easily – they would call my attitude by their *cliché* 'over-reacting'. But Oman and G.N. Clark always resented their being turned down by New College, normally enough. Celtic temperaments differ from English. Further rejections from second-rate humans followed. It did not console me that those second-rate dons would soon be forgotten. It was only later, after further experiences from ordinary humans, that I recognised the truth of Shakespeare's reflection: every set-back at their hands proved an advantage from which I greatly profited. I should have been grateful, though not to them, for I knew their motives: it was as if there were a guardian angel at the gate, forbidding me to go any other way than to fulfil my own true nature.

So I went my own way, under my own control, teaching where and as much as I liked, probably too much for my own good. Out of the ordinary ruck and run I had some exceptional pupils, two or three even became professors. Neville Williams followed me into the Tudor period; John Armstrong of Hertford became a noted medievalist who brought to light new evidence on Richard III's usurpation. Veronica Wedgwood and I became intimate friends, encouraging one another's work.

My ablest pupil was John Cooper of Magdalen: a psychotic case, he refused to go to C.S. Lewis for tutorials in political theory, and Magdalen asked me to take him on. He had had a bad war, graduating to the height of lance-corporal. He was by way of being a Trotskyist; since I was well read in Marxism I could cope with him, and treated him sympathetically. His essays were the best ever read to me, and discussions would go on for two or more hours. Of course he got a First, after groaning that it was out of the question. Then he moaned that he could not possibly compete for an All Souls Fellowship. Of course he won it. When he came into College he made himself a perfect nuisance. He wouldn't speak to the senior Fellows; and, with the other ex-wartime juniors, proto-hippies – Isaiah Berlin called them laughingly the '*sans-culottes*', though they were no laughing matter – Cooper's psychosis enabled him to collect a Cave of Adullam which opposed anything and everybody, especially me. My ablest pupil became my constant opponent. Fortunately, Trinity took him on as a tutor: there he became not only an upholder of tradition but a positive reactionary, and died young. Clearly there was something wrong with him.

Examining for the Higher School Certificate was a quick, if boring, way of making some extra money – for which I stayed on into the summer vacations, when my contemporaries – Pares, Connolly, Quennell, Hudson, David Cecil, Uncle Tom Cobleigh and all – were enjoying themselves all over the Continent. I was recruited also to examine for the Diploma in Politics (yet again) and Economics.

This preliminary examination was a simple affair, below the standard of Final Schools. Two memories only of it I have now. Lionel Robbins, who had a spell teaching economics at New College, set a paper that was so advanced as to be almost post-graduate. This piece of hubris, to show how clever he was, showed very little judgment, for few people could answer the questions. And how could one rate them? The second was the appearance as an examinee of a daughter of Sir Charles Trevelyan, Labour Minister of Education. She had already been ploughed once, and made a poor showing again. At her viva she was quite brash with her young examiner, and I found myself blushing. Ploughed again, she was sent down and went off to Cambridge.

For myself I went on with my historical reading, gradually closing in on the Tudor period. In reading for Schools I leaned rather to the nineteenth century, was always interested in French history and literature – and still am. (I have just read the whole fifteen volumes of Saint-Beuve's *Causeries du Lundi* and his *Cahier*.) Consulting E.L. Woodward, whose field this was, as to my future work, he advised me away from it into the sixteenth century. The point was not lost upon young Berlin, already sophisticated, standing by: he was amused as always by the human spectacle. By good luck I settled for the sixteenth century, where there was then little competition, against the nineteenth where there was so much. On the other hand, in Oxford there was little help or encouragement. A.F. Pollard, who led in that field in London, rarely came down to College, and was not at all forthcoming when he did.

Pollard was not a companionable man. I had the impression that he was rather disregarded by the grandees – his manner was lower-middle-class. He had done a fine job in establishing the History School in London University and the Institute of Historical Research. He expected to be made Regius Professor of Modern History at Oxford in succession to Sir Charles Firth. I was disappointed that he was not. But I never got much out of *him* in talk, as with most of the obliging old boys. Once, when we discussed Henry VIII, whose biography he had written, he stuck to the official line as to Anne Boleyn's guilt. I did not then know enough to question it, though I now know that it was completely false: poor Anne was simply framed. Thomas Cromwell had to do the dirty work, the wickedest thing he ever did.

Pollard was an imperceptive, insensitive type, bent on constitutional minutiae, indeed very good at them – not my line. I was interested in biography, understanding personality, which was not only unfashionable then, but looked down upon by the professionals. Unimaginative of them. Once again I took my own line and worked on alone.

My chief encouragement continued to be, even more than it had been at Christ Church, in talks with David Cecil.

Now we were both dons (he was teaching English Literature and History at Wadham) he came to visit me at all hours – and suggested that I keep a bottle of sherry. It had never occurred to me. He had sat for the Fellowship examination, like his uncles Robert and Hugh – none of them got in. David could not face the ordeal of the viva in front of the assembled Fellows; when confronted by the paper of pieces to translate he didn't attempt even the French (as I had done), but fled from the room.

However, when I survived the ordeal, he kindly said, 'If you have any trouble with all those knives and forks and glasses at dinner, I'll tell you.' Actually, my table manners were better than his, or of some of the others – for instance, Cruttwell's, unkindly described by his pupil, Evelyn Waugh. As for Gerald Berners, a later friend, he said in his peer's falsetto that he had been taught as a child *what* to eat but not *how* to eat it. The sainted Dominican Gervase Mathew – Graham Greene's spiritual adviser (not to much point) – simply plastered the food over his face, an embarrassing guest at meals.

❖

After this academic excursus let us come to the life in College. After all anyone can write up its history from the documents, but few have lived it.

All institutions have their customs, their idiosyncrasies and totems. Ours was the Mallard, printed and depicted on everything, silver, china, etc. as the Cardinal's Hat was at Christ Church. When All Souls was a-building a wild duck, a mallard, had flown up from the marshy ground. The cult of the Mallard was invented. Wild duck, mitigated by orange salad, appeared on the menu (our menus were in French) at the annual All Souls Gaudy, November 2. In my simple way I keep the commemoration of that day still, wherever I may be, usually alone.[2]

The College was founded for service to Church and State, and to pray for the souls of the Founder and the faithful departed in the Hundred Years' War. Until the Reformation we had been in part a chantry; in the ante-Chapel there was room for half-a-dozen altars for masses. The College had dragged its feet, until a Protestant archbishop ordered it to sell mass-vestments and such gear, and invest the proceeds more remuneratively in land. Only the converted Morrah had a mass said for the old souls; we contented ourselves with saying the Founder's prayers.

The Lord Mallard was head of the junketings in Common Room after dinner in Hall. He was not elected or appointed, but arrived at by a sort of afflatus, as some Popes had arrived at St Peter's chair, by 'inspiration' of the Holy Ghost. To come down to earth, the Lord Mallard was he who had the best voice to sing the Mallard Song. For years this was Lang, who could sing the song better than anybody; in my time it was Dougie Malcolm; after him decline set in.

The Mallard Song was an appalling piece of seventeenth-century doggerel, and I listened to it dutifully not without some embarrassment. Nobody else was embarrassed, but by this time they were all jolly, in liquor, while this tee-totaller kept a cool head, half in and half out of the proceedings. Another sceptical mind, Woodward, used to catch my eye, to see how I was taking it. I moved my lips loyally in the chorus, while the others roared out till the rafters rung:

> O by the blood of King Edward,
> O by the blood of King Edward,
> It *was* a swapping, swa-a-apping mallard!

The King Edward must have been Edward VI, and the

---

[2] See my poem, 'All Souls Night in Wyoming', on pp.201–3 below.

tune runs in my head to this day. I used to think it might be a parody of the Litany. Anyhow the company gave themselves up to it heartily, unselfconsciously; the servants could hear us roaring away in the Hall. I have always been baffled by the unselfconsciousness of *l'homme moyen sensuel*. Morrah always got drunk, but he was light-headed anyway. An adherent of the White Rose, he recognised the Stuart descendant, Crown Prince Rupprecht of Bavaria, as Robert II of England, Robert III of Scotland. I thought that silly – he took it seriously.

And the words, the words of the song!! –

> Griffin, Bustard, Turkey, Capon,
> Let other hungry mortals gape on.
> And on their bones with stomach fall hard –
> But let All Souls men have their Mallard.

Then we came in, with O by the blood of King Edward, etc.

> The Romans once admired a Gander
> More than they did their best Commander,
> Because he saved, if some don't fool us,
> The place that's named from the skull of Tolus.

O, by the blood of King Edward, etc.

> The poets feigned Jove turned a Swan,
> But let them prove it if they can –
> As for our proofs 'tis not at all hard,
> It was a swapping, swapping Mallard.

There then came a verse in the original that was omitted in deference to Lang's clerical cloth – about the Mallard's 'swapping great organ of generation'. The seventeenth century was not so nice about these things as the Victorians.

Then let us drink and dance a Galliard
All to the memory of the Mallard,
And as the Mallard doth in pool
Let's dabble, duck, and dive in bowl.

– O by the blood of King Edward,
O by the blood of King Edward,
It was a swapping, swa-a-apping Mallard.

While this was going on, and I took my modest part in the proceedings, I would wonder how long it was since a bustard had appeared on the tables in Hall. Not since the seventeenth century itself, I dare say; it appears in Pepys's Diary at City banquets, but I think the big bird had vanished from East Anglian heaths by the next century. And how long was it since we had danced a galliard round the Hall? Not since the seventeenth century either, I expect. Up to 1914 there had been 'cock-fighting' on the tables, i.e. Fellows doubled up, jostling and bouncing each other off, until at one Gaudy Pollard was bounced off and broke his leg. The War put an end to that sport, along with much else.

At the end of the Song there arose a roar of rapping on the tables until the roof rang again. Healths were drunk in traditional fashion. Two enormous silver cups progressed down the tables. One stood up, a Fellow on either side, to protect one while drinking, bowed to one's opposite number across the table and passed the cup on according to the ritual. Even I could not avoid a sip of this, a specially concocted spicy drink, not bad to the taste.

We then progressed into the crowded Common Room for dessert, port and more drinking, speeches. And more singing. Baker-Wilbraham, a long-nosed, lugubrious-looking baronet, who was Chancellor of half the dioceses in England, was a Devonshireman. So he sang:

Tom Pearce, Tom Pearce, lend me your grey mare,
All along, down along, out along lea,
For I want for to go to Widdicombe Fair,
With Bill Brewer, Jan Stewer, Peter Gurney, Peter
    Davy, Dan'l Whiddon, Harry Hawke,
Old Uncle Tom Cobleigh and all.

Then we joined in, with 'Uncle Tom Cobleigh and all.' Oman, who had written a vast book about the Peninsular War, sang a song about 'the bloody Albuera'. We were not so well up in that, though the Codrington possessed all the papers of Sir Charles Vaughan, diplomat there throughout, which would have told us. Swinton, as Major General familiar with the recent war in France – and indeed an inventor of the Tank – chimed in with a song from his Mess:

Gentille Alouette, Gentille Alouette –
A la gorge, à la jambe –

I forget how it went, but on and on.

Our chef, Arnott, himself a Freeman of Oxford with ancient rights on Port Meadow, had been chef to a French General during the war, so we had the most scrumptious food in those days. Each Fellow in residence was steward for a week in turn, and this was an education for a tyro brought up on working-class fare. I still remember some of his splendid confections. I also reflect now, ungratefully, that all this grand food was not the thing for a young duodenal. I would have done better to go to bed with a bowl of bread and milk – which was Lloyd George's peasant taste as against boring public banquets. However, this was not on the cards at All Souls.

Lunch was a simpler affair in our beautiful buttery, for I think that in previous days, when dinner was at an earlier hour, Fellows had a snack from the cold meats from the day before. Breakfast in Common Room was Victorian, and huge: not only bacon and eggs but kidneys and mushrooms, smoked haddock and kedgeree, kippers and a cold ham. David Cecil told me that a large fresh ham regularly appeared on the side-board at Hatfield, and was not seen again – so many servants to feed. In the Thirties our breakfast fare much diminished; anyway, I settled for a boiled egg, and have stuck to that all my life. And living on top of one of the best cellars in Oxford meant nothing to me.

The dark-panelled Common Room, with polished mahogany tables reflecting the candle-light, was dominated by a bust of Wren over the big chimney piece. There was a splendid screen of hammered and figured leather to keep out draughts – external ones. The Georgian window has a noble view across the lawn to the Roman dome of Gibbs's Radcliffe Camera.

The buttery, though small, was the most original room in Oxford: a coffered ceiling, an extravagant marvel of geometry as an oval dome, of the architect Hawksmoor. Of him we possessed the only portrait bust, looking down on us from his niche – the opposite niche occupied by a bust of the Georgian manciple of his day. Here, in the capacious closet beneath that rustic bust, we kept T.E. Lawrence's ceremonial Arab robes. These always proved a lure for visitors and guests whom we had to entertain. There was the splendid burnous of gold and silver woven tissue – many are the shoulders I have tried it on: it must have engulfed his diminutive figure. His head-dress was held together by gold filigree hammered out of the sovereigns which had helped on the Arab Revolt against the Turks. Then there were his sandals, and the diamond ring which his friend the Emir Feisal gave him. It was like T.E.L.'s perversity not to attach importance to possessions: he had not bothered to hold on to the robes he had worn at the Paris Conference – by way of not attracting attention.

Lawrence had lived in a very spartan way in College, not coming down to meals but sustaining himself on biscuits and dried fruit, figs and raisins. His room in the old quad was sparsely furnished; mainly cushions on the floor, Arab-like. There he wrote away at his book. Late at night he would descend into the smoking-room to chat. Over the Middle East he was engaged in controversy with a very superior former Fellow, no less a person than Curzon. Defeated in his Arab hopes, he threatened to present two peacocks, 'George' and 'Nathaniel', to preen themselves about the big quadrangle.

The manciple, Chaucerian title, was head of the servants and presided in the Buttery from his pew, original panelling all around. He presided too over the brewing of the College audit (i.e. old) ale, famous for its double strength, liable to knock the unaware out. It never knocked me out, for I only once tasted the stuff, an All Souls speciality. The young F.E. Smith, who was not an All Souls man, had once invaded the buttery, demanded a beaker of Old Ale, and had it put down to his rival at the Bar, John Simon. so like F.E.'s notorious impertinence!

Though Simon was a noted All Souls figure in the public eye, we did not see much of him in those years. He was too busy in London making a fortune at the Bar, and in politics trying to make up for the appalling mistake he had made in resigning from Asquith's government over Conscription in 1916. He had been deeply wrong, even over the moral issue which he placed first – like the Nonconformist he was. France was being bled white by the Germans, it was intolerable that Britain should not share the burden in manpower. Secondly, within Britain, the voluntary system meant that a high proportion of the best young men, especially officers, were killed off early in the war.

Simon had not the imagination to appreciate this. Moreover, he was a Little Englander, with no knowledge of Europe or European history, let alone of Germany and her record of successful aggression with Bismarck. Simon was not alone in this ignorance, witness the disastrous ignorance of the Men of the Thirties, Baldwin, Neville Chamberlain, Halifax, and so many others.

In College Simon's mate, i.e. elected together, was L.S. Amery. There could not be a greater contrast, intellectually and even physically: Simon tall and elegant, holding himself gracefully, always self-consciously; Amery small and squat, ugly and forceful, compact of muscle and punch. Amery had moved about the world, had been in the South African war, and even knew Europe, which few people at the top in politics did. The importance of this comes out in the indefensible record the Men of the Thirties had in the conduct of Britain's foreign policy all through the decade. Amery, a good Tory, had a better record than anyone in opposing it and foreseeing the fatal consequences.

Simon's mistaken desertion not only was decisive for his career – broke it in two – but is no less revealing of what was wrong with his political outlook, the restrictedness, the lack of knowledge of the world as it really is. To say that it was that of a Liberal Nonconformist Little Englander from the lower-middle-class is enough: that defines it.

At the early juncture Amery put his finger on the trouble with his mate, saw into it. 'You and the political principles and traditions you most cherish have come up against the facts of a new world which is incompatible with them. Whatever their intrinsic truth they have no real relation to the facts of today – or of many years past. The peculiar conserving effects of our party system have kept them politically alive for more than a generation after their time. But the last ten years have been, not the herald of some great advance, but the last backwash of a tide that has run out.'

What a penetrating diagnosis that is! How it puts paid to the Liberal illusions based on their victory in 1906 (really a reaction from the Boer War), and accounts for the collapse of the careers of so many good men launched upon those hopes! Simon's mate pointed the moral for him. 'Don't be tempted by our feelings to throw yourself henceforward into a campaign of opposition to all the inevitable changes that the new order of things will bring with it during the War and after the War. Sit down and think the world out for yourself anew. Become for a few years a dispassionate student of the Empire's and the world's affairs ...'

In the event Simon lost his faith and convictions; but his early restricted origins made it impossible for him to open out into a wider view. On the other hand this diagnosis shows the originality and independence of Amery's mind – underestimated in his own day and now forgotten. (One reason was that he was a dull speaker – lively only in private conversation.)

What was wrong with Simon? Everybody was sure that there was something wrong, but nobody could diagnose it. The impeccable trained intellect was a machine, it worked automatically, as I have observed it in a College meeting. My mate, Roger Makins, made three points in a nervous youthful speech. When he came to sum up he forgot the third point. Simon, from the top table, where he did not appear to be listening, automatically supplied it. Donald Somervell, not in the same class with Simon, could imitate his technique in opening a case. First, several sentences of a deluding simplicity, then slip a fast one in! No wonder Simon had little respect for the Bar, where he was an acknowledged leader.

His personality was inhibited, if not crippled, by his Nonconformist origins. He could not let himself go, he could not be natural and spontaneous. The geniality was deliberate, and everybody therefore thought it bogus – calling people by their Christian name, and getting it wrong. There was a vein of disingenuousness, which clever people could see through and thought hypocritical. His junior colleagues among the lawyers had many stories of his fallible – they thought it false – personal touch. (Later on, he shamelessly flattered Neville Chamberlain's ludicrous vanity.)

2. Warden Pember

Cyril Radcliffe used to have a story of Simon proposing to Mrs Ronald Greville, on his knees in her drawing room in Charles Street. That illegitimate brewing millionairess – a strong proponent of Appeasement – had bigger fish to fry, as one of Edward VII's women. No hopes there, Simon found a second wife who, being Irish, became an alcoholic. At the grand parties in the big quad at Encaenia one used to see him – patient, courteous, controlled as ever – leading her pathetically by the hand. By then he was High Steward of the university, 'nothing to do, and £5 a year'.

Always careful about money, as about everything, he did ask us all out to lunch at Fritwell, his Jacobean mansion near Banbury. When he sacrificed his £50,000 a year for politics, he sold the place. I have an early memory of his appearing one day unexpectedly in the middle of the week. When asked in buttery what brought him down: 'To advise Sir William Morris [of Morris Motors] how to get out of his income-tax.'

Among customs or duties, which had the subsidiary effect of forwarding one's education, was the annual plate-count. This took place in the autumn. The two long tables in Hall were heaped with the accumulations of silver and plate since the Civil War. Hardly anything from before that date had survived, for the College had emptied itself of its resources for the cause of Church and King.

Thus the only medieval specimens were the Founder's Salt and a couple of maser bowls. These were of historic importance, and priceless value, for their rarity. The Salt is of fifteenth-century German workmanship: the figure of a huntsman carrying the crystal container on his head, at his feet a diminutive hunt of figures, animals, in enamel. This rather fragile piece was brought out to stand before the Warden at the All Souls Gaudy. The maser bowls of polished maple wood, with silver gilt rims, made no other appearance – we did not drink from them.

The tables groaned under the candelabra and candlesticks which lighted our meals; dozens of Georgian, with earlier and later, wine jugs, beakers, tumblers. There were the silver teapots which, in those select days, appeared on our individual tea-trays in the smoking-room. Some oddities bespoke the difference between Georgian and (late) Victorian taste. One hideous object was a big spread of silver-tipped stag's horns, inlaid in the centre a snuff-box. Ungainly and ugly, it was never used – I suppose some Victorian sportsman's joke.

There were small snuff-boxes, regularly in use at dessert (not by me); flagons, altar vessels, and ugly equipment for the distasteful habit of smoking, Victorian cigar boxes. On Gaudy nights the atmosphere in the confined space of the smoking room was unbreathable – thank goodness there was the coffee room (no smoking) to retire into. One small improvement to be grateful for, in otherwise deplorable days, is that there is far less smoking. Victorians – with their actual *cult* of smoking! – had no idea how bad it was for them.

Mountains of good cutlery, of course. I have reason to remember those fine heavy tea-spoons. One summer, to help my former pupil Veronica Wedgwood, who was President of the P.E.N. Club, I gave a tea-party in the Hall. An international gathering of just over a hundred members turned up: at the end one Georgian tea-spoon, only one, was missing. I have sometimes wondered where, or in what country, it may turn up – it would have our coat-of-arms on it.

One little box was of perhaps nostalgic interest. It was covered in Stuart, or perhaps Elizabethan, embroidery and contained a few pathetic reminders of the Founder, Archbishop Chichele. One was a kind of jewelled nut that may have topped a mitre; there was a little crystal cross, and some semi-precious object from a vestment, a cope or something. I should have remembered better, for among the traditional sinecures handed down to us, I held that of Cus. Joc. (Custos Jocalium).

Then there was wine-tasting, an informal affair which the domestic bursar held along with the Domestic Committee, of which residents in College were usually members. I can't have been much use at this. Actually All Souls did not have the best cellar in Oxford, for Grant Robertson, domestic bursar for years, had not been much interested. On the other hand, undiscriminating guzzlers of port can hardly be expected to have the best palates: at Oriel it was said that this distinction was reserved to the abstemious Newman.

Naturally the best cellars were built up where there was someone who made it their special subject. In my time this was supposed to be Pembroke College, which enjoyed the delectable authority of Dr Ramsden, of whom John Betjeman wrote the touching – and so true – memorial poem:

> Dr Ramsden cannot read *The Times* obituary today,
>   He's dead …
> Those old cheeks that faintly flushed as the port suffused
>   the veins,
>   Drained white.

I don't suppose that our chief devotee of port, Professor Holdsworth, had an exquisite palate, any more than Professor Blackstone, whose composition of the *Commentaries on the Laws of England* was 'invigorated and supported in the fatigue by the temperate use of a bottle of port'. His complexion, to judge from his portrait, looked like it. So did Holdsworth's.

❖

My first manciple, one Wright, was a grim Presbyterian Scot, a disciplinarian who had been brought up at Victorian Balmoral. He did not like the junior Fellows, and could not approve of me, a confessed Labour man. In the General Strike of 1926 I ought, in his view, to have left College to help the strike-breakers. When I left College for the Acland Home instead and a dangerous operation, he rather came round – too late for me. His successor, an old soldier who had lost a leg in the war, was more human, a kind man. And *his* successor as manciple, Bert Watson, became a life-long, dear friend. In late years he and his wife used to stay with me at Trenarren. He had a devotion to the Scilly Isles, and gave me rare sub-tropical echiums from there, which will grow in our sheltered, southward-looking garden, especially in the 'Manciple's Patch'.

The coffee room was a Victorian adjunct to give shelter from the atmosphere of the smoking-room, which became unbreathable with smoke on Gaudy nights. I cherished the privacy and quiet of that inner sanctum, hung with photographs and a few drawings, of former Fellows. There were the six Fellows killed in the 1914-1918 War, two of them legendary: the strong, masculine features of the Prime Minister's eldest son, Raymond Asquith; the sharp features of Shaw-Stewart, whose legendary brilliance people still spoke of. He had been one of that gilded generation at Balliol, to whom Ronnie Knox belonged – and led a widowered life thereafter, for almost all were killed. There too were Foster Cunliffe, and a Radcliffe, from his Devonshire manor; and Anderson in uniform, gay and smiling, only a boy.

I had a private cult of these dead Fellows I had never known. I can't explain it, no one knew of it, but I felt their absence. It would be sentimental to say that the College had been wounded, but we were a small society, and they were missing. When one goes round larger Oxford and Cambridge colleges, or the London clubs, there are the hundreds of names the country sorely missed – how cruelly in the Thirties when their leadership was needed! To me, living so much in the world of poetry and imagination, these men were not absent. I grieved for them, but they were in mind.

Another photograph attracted me, that of T.E. Lawrence, also in army uniform. Though I used to hear about him, and Lionel Curtis was his chief friend, I met him only once, the night his Fellowship expired. He would dare-devil drive on his motor-bike from camp, arrive in the night, sleep a few hours and away early before we got up. That Gaudy night the smoking-room was crowded with people in white ties and tails – the rule then (on ordinary nights black ties and dinner jackets and I could change in 5 to 7 minutes. Some juniors took three-quarters of an hour to dress in the mornings – and never wrote their masterpieces of research.) Suddenly there arrived a slim boyish figure in RAF corporal's uniform. He might have been a boy of eighteen or nineteen, slimmest of waists, but for the mad Irish eyes and the tortured mouth.

A fine engraving of a handsome Regency buck caught my eye. This was the diplomat Charles Augustus Murray, whose biography lay in the bookcase below. The College folklore about him would have enticed Lytton Strachey's attention for his *Queen Victoria*, if he had known it. Murray, when young, was a gentleman-in-waiting at Court and, with his looks, was bound to attract the regard of the ladies. It was said that the unfortunate Lady Flora Hastings was in love with him. One night at Windsor, at a little game of whist, wary old Lord Melbourne dropped a card and looked down, to see the Queen's little foot resting on the broad patent leather shoe of young Murray. The sage Melbourne decided that it was time to marry Victoria safely off to her cousin Albert.

Murray was the grandson of the last royal governor of Virginia, Lord Dunmore. His American career is of the highest interest: he was the first person to travel with the Pawnee Indians, and wrote a classic *Travels in North America*. There was a romantic side to his story over there. By a piece of serendipity I was able, years later, to work out the sinister end to it, the mysterious death of his son in an Atlantic crossing.[3]

Across from him was a photograph of Viceroy Chelmsford. We had living with us an old Anglo-Indian, Sir Henry Sharp, skin like leather creased and crackled by Indian sun, with a dry laugh spaced on three notes, no sense of humour. He had been Secretary of the Viceroy, or the Viceroy's Council, and was now Secretary to the university's Statutory Commission. He always addressed Chelmsford with the vice-regal 'Sir'. One day the smoking-room door opened and in came that fine, rather noble figure. I had never set eyes on a peer of the realm before – ten a penny today – and the aggressive young proletarian was suitably impressed. I was still more impressed to be told that our grandees were never to be addressed by their titles or offices, but simply by their surnames: in the institution which was our home we were all equals.

Our military Fellow, Major-General Sir Ernest Swinton, found this hard to understand: used to discipline, he found it hard to take from young men; he had to learn. And found it impossible to learn academic dress, just when we wore gowns, or gowns plus hoods, or surplices in Chapel with or without hoods, according to the liturgical season. We tumbled to it by instinct, but could not explain it by rote to him. When young Quintin Hogg complained of the hardness of the College beds – they were iron-hard and the Victorian Fellows never noticed – Swinton was affronted and called Hogg a 'sissy' (Quintin of all people!) When he,

[3] See 'The Romantic Story of Charles Augustus Murray', in my *Portraits and Views*.

the General, had been a cadet at Sandhurst, the young had to race naked across the yard to their morning's cold *douche*.

This was not for us. But really the old domestic arrangements *were* bleak. There was no w.c. on my staircase. Sometimes I was sick at night, would wrap myself in woolly dressing gown and rug, to descend into the quad and along to the draughty passage where the loos were. 'Public splendour, private squalor' – Cyril Radcliffe one winter got congestion of the lungs up in his arctic/attic bedroom across from me. Gradually we were up-dated.

Meanwhile what could be more cosy than tea-time and chat around the smoking-room fire, each then with separate tea-tray and silver teapot. There would be dear Richard Pares and Geoffrey Hudson; David Cecil would often appear as my guest. He and Richard could talk Jane Austen to their hearts' content, recognising characters from the novels as old acquaintances from schooldays, Eton and Winchester. I did not graduate to Jane Austen until middle age – she had not been heard of in my native village of Tregonissey.

Bird-like Reggie Harris was a fountain of mirth and naughty jokes. Though a nephew of the Pragmatist philosopher, F.C.S. Schiller of Corpus, he had had a brief spell as a Roman convert. So, taking the mantelpiece for altar, he could recite bits of the missal as a French priest would intone, *per saecula saeculorum*, pronounced to rhyme with *rhume*. Or it would be this exchange:

A young acolyte: 'Father, what is the most holy thing ever lost?'
Priest: 'My son, the holy prepuce.'

Or a rhyme of the young Sorbonniens:

Je *hais* les tours de Saint Sulpice:

Quand par hasard je les rencontre,
Je pisse
Contre.

A brilliant linguist, he was as fluent in colloquial Latin. Looking out across the lawn at the manciple fumbling with the big, decorative wrought-iron gate, it would be, 'O mancipule, quid agis?'

His German streak made him very musical – which, for the most part, our seniors were decidedly not. So Reggie could sing bits from the B minor Mass, or *Messiah*, with the declaration that Handel was 'the great master of the common chord'. I missed Reggie's fun so much when he left College for an oddly divagatory career: leader-writer on the *Times*, railway director in Argentina, economic dictator in Iceland during the second War. In that he had an appalling accident at, of all places, Capua. So he could say that he had indeed 'met his Capua'. It damaged him permanently, and he lost his old gaiety. For all his gifts, he was endearingly naive.

Some of the seniors contributed their fun. Oman's memories went back a long way. He had seen Napoleon III and the Empress Eugénie on the terrace of the Tuileries, watching their little son, the spirited Prince Imperial, drilling his squad of cadets. The Emperor prematurely aged and crumpled up, the Empress radiant in a zebra-striped crinoline. Then came the thunderbolt of the Franco-Prussian war. Oman saw the victorious, but deleterious, Prussians – the Emperor William, Bismarck and Moltke – riding abreast into Frankfort, to not much of a welcome, for the city was Southern, anti-Prussian.

Myself, I can never forgive the dastardly Commune of 1871 for burning down the Renaissance palace of the Tuileries. Whenever in the gardens there I always deplore the vast gap between the Pavillon Flore and the Pavillon Marsan. The idiot populace can destroy, but it cannot construct – except under direction.

Grant Robertson, good man, was a compulsive talker and regarded as a bore. But he was an interesting bore and when – in the second War he gave himself up to 'the sickness of hope deferred' and despaired – I could get him on to his old acquaintance among the lady novelists. Craster told me that he had been an Edwardian 'masher', kid gloves and all. He had known the redoubtable Rhoda Broughton in Holywell, who was thought so 'advanced', for she smoked. At our grand Encaenia Luncheon he would have as his guest Marie Corelli, over from Stratford: a plump little figure dressed in white muslin like a girl of seventeen, large blue sash over protuberant behind. *O sancta simplicitas!*

No one was supposed to know that Robertson had committed the indiscretion of two novels, under the romantic name of Wymond Carey. He never owned up to them. One of them was called *Love the Judge*; but I never learned whether this meant 'Love, the Judge' or was an adjuration to love the Judge. Even Cosmo Lang had perpetrated an early novel, a Stuart romance of the *Little Lord Fauntleroy* kind. So perhaps I might be forgiven for sowing my wild oats with *Politics and the Younger Generation*. Poetry I for long kept to myself.

There had been a tradition of College walks; I came in at the tail-end of this. The Victorians were great walkers; G.M. Trevelyan had twice walked the whole coast of Cornwall, and once walked from Cambridge to Oxford, 83 miles, within 24 hours. Already the environs were being built up, all the way out to Cowley, owing to Morris and his motor works, a dominant feature on our horizon. We were becoming the Latin Quarter of Morris-Cowley; even the railway station had a placard announcing 'Oxford: the Place where Morris Cars are made.' A junior Fellow found himself in a railway compartment with two enlightened young ladies. One breathed enthusiastically: 'Oxford! That's the place! There's a smashin' Woolworth's there!'

Afternoons Richard Pares and I would go slumming in historic St Ebbe's, where the famous medieval friars, Roger Bacon and company, had lived – now obliterated by a monstrous shopping centre for the populace. Wystan Auden preferred the squalid canal banks, where the gasometers were. Further afield we would go up-river to Binfield with its holy well, or up Boar's Hill where the poets lived then, Bridges, Masefield, Robert Graves, Robert Nicholls. Autumn was the time for Woodstock and the park at Blenheim, to see the leaves turning in the serried ranks of avenues, like the great Duke's military formations.

One could still walk through Jowett's Parks out along the Cherwell into Mesopotamia, on to Marston with Cromwell's House, where G.N. Clark lived then. Along the way was a stopping place with a stile, where I would sit when alone and write down the poem that ran in my head. How well I remember the spot, and the little stream that ran there too! One last collective walk took us out across the fields to ruined Kidlington, where Lionel Curtis lived by the river.

He gave us all lunch, memorable for a typical Headlam explosion. Curtis had married his secretary, daughter of a small Devon cleric, her baptismal name of Gladys abolished for Patricia. She made the mistake of calling on the Bishop to say grace. Headlam hesitated, said it, then exploded: 'In the first place, I am not your chaplain; in the second, it is your husband's place to say grace in his own household.' Secretly, I was not sorry to see her put down. For this conventional, lower-middle-class secretary, hearing me spoken of as a proletarian Leftist, described me as a 'peasant', which was far from the case. With her rich, rather sexy voice she had no sense of humour.

Back in College were the customs kept up, pleasant and unpleasant. Pleasantest was the Beating of the Bounds on Ascension day. The bounds of St Mary's parish ran through the middle of the College. So the clergy from St Mary's, churchwardens and sidesmen arrived with their traditional canes, to beat knowledge of the bounds into the choirboys in their cassocks. We threw them coppers for which they scrabbled on the lawn; then they all went in for a glorious feed in the Hall.

First-year Fellows had been Probationers; this had only just been dropped, though Roger Makins and I lived in the Probationers' rooms in the Old Quad. We were supposed to make, or stir, the salads in Hall before Sunday dinner. I was no good at that – salads had never appeared on the kitchen table at Tregonissey. Worse was the chore of being 'Screw'. The junior Fellow dining, at dessert for which we processed to Common Room, sat at the bottom of the table by the door to replenish the decanters as the jugs of wine came in. I hated this job. By the time I had decanted the port into the claret, or into my sleeve, the utility of the tradition was questionable. 'Screw' was not supposed to leave the room until the seniors, sopping up their port, had all finished and left. They sat on and on. I used to think that Holdsworth's voluminous *History of English Law* was solidified All Souls port; for after glass after glass he would go to his room and write regularly till midnight.

On they sat at the head of the table; mutinous, I would be bidden up. Nine o'clock – the butler, poor old Ryder, would be scrabbling at the door, longing to clear the room and get home to his wife. Did they never think of the servants? I decided to take my courage in my hands and leave my post. This was not well seen, contrary to tradition, but I hope I ended it.

My own scout, Welsted, I shared with Simon, of whom he was terrified. When Simon was coming for the week-end, Welsted would be all of a dither, a nervous wreck, a big fat rabbit. I could not understand it, but I think that the 'Impeccable' – Asquith's name for him – was not one for suffering fools gladly. By his standards ordinary humans were all very peccable.

Best it is to remember those autumn evenings by the fireside with friends in the smoking-room, or in my own dark-panelled room looking out on the Warden's garden on one side, St Mary's spire on the other. Leaves turning on the great mounded chestnut trees, lights coming out across the gardens in the long range of Queen's, the bells of New College ringing for evensong, and then further off, over the roofs, those of Magdalen.

It is all in my Journals and Poems, even in my pocket notebooks; for, queasy with regular returns of ulcer, I too had fears that I 'might cease to be' and wanted to catch every moment of life on the wing. This had become my home, of my work, my friends, my imagination. My heart turns over at remembering it all.

CHAPTER 3

The Thirties

My head was turned by politics. I cannot blame All Souls, though the College was part of it, for that was its inflexion, public affairs in its widest meaning and with an overriding sense of responsibility. From the older Fellows I gathered the sense of the priority of duty and public service. They would do anything that they thought was their duty, they took it for granted. Simon, the highest paid leader of the Bar, would decline a brief worth hundreds for a miserable political meeting anywhere. He told Asquith, in declining to be Lord Chancellor, that he hated the law – that was odd, when he had a genius for it. Cyril Radcliffe, ablest of our younger lawyers, who might have been a Liberal or even Labour Lord Chancellor, gave up his remunerative legal career, for public service on numerous royal commissions, notably that for partitioning India and creating Pakistan.

The time itself, for anyone historically-minded, turned one to politics. After the slaughter and destruction, the damage to civilisation itself – initiating the age of violence and terrorism – of the first German war, there was a burst of idealism. Hope was really in the air. We believed in internationalism and peace.

For myself, I thought that, since the upper classes of Europe had made war, the only foundation for international peace was the international working-classes. This was optimistic, but it was not unreasonable: it was the view of the noble Jaurès and Léon Blum, of Ramsay MacDonald before he lost his faith, no less than of Marx and Lenin. No hope anywhere else anyway. I became a fanatic.

This was the background of the Politics book I was writing, along with teaching political theory. The second element in it, hardly less important to me, was disillusionment with the Old Men of Europe who had made such a mess of it – no hope from them. They had sacrificed the generation immediately before me – there were the photographs of them on the walls, though I needed no reminding. So I saw the only hope in my own generation, to which – ingenuous as ever – I sought to give a lead. Hence the book became *Politics and the Younger Generation*. (Habakkuk told me years later that they were ready to follow its lead anywhere.)

I don't want to write about it here, simply about its background in College. I had been hammering away at its themes in conversation with Pares and Hudson, sometimes even with the hostile Woodward, bent on putting me down. No doubt I was uppish, I had a message to put across; but he was pompous, and had a higher opinion of himself than I had of him. He was singular in taking quite the wrong line with an acutely sensitive youngster, unsophisticated and terribly wrought up. When I came through my troubles, and my books were successful, he became envious. Fancy that, from a patronising senior! He wrote an autobiography, called *Short Journey*. An old woman at Trinity, Cambridge, 'Granny' Gow, much preferred it to *A Cornish Childhood*: he thought it more 'urbane'. I was neither urbane, nor urban, let alone suburban as Woodward was. His book had no success; *A Cornish Childhood* has sold half-a-million copies and is living to this day.

Geoffrey Faber was willing to publish my Politics book, and T.S. Eliot conscientiously took his sharp pencil to it. I have described the process in an article about him as a publisher in the *Yale Literary Review*. Eliot came down to

3. The Thirties

All Souls: I can see him now, sitting on the hard leather sofa in the smoking-room, the neat clerical appearance, pencil poised, the care and kindness. He did not seem to disapprove. R.C.K. Ensor, an earlier non-election from our examination, did. He thought it much inferior to G.D.H. Cole's *World of Labour*. But it was a totally different kind of book, not comparable. Cole's was a factual survey of Trade Unions, statistics, what not. Not a statistic in mine; it was a Politics book, an ideological manifesto.

The financial crisis of 1931 coincided with its publication, and killed the book stone dead. Just my luck, I thought: it added to the glow of resentment burning within me.

Meanwhile I had let myself in for fighting an uphill struggle as a Labour candidate in the hopeless Liberal-and-Nonconformist dominated, backward county of Cornwall. Fancy the foolery – there could never be a Liberal government again; the Party was a corpse encumbering the ground; a waste of one's vote to vote. 'If you wuz a Liberal you'd get in flyin',' said one wiseacre. I knew that – but what an escape! The Election was a disaster for the Labour Party: 55 MPs, against the 'National' majority of 550, who could have done whatever was necessary in the interest of the nation in that hopeless decade.

The historian has always thought that 1931 was decisive, a parting of the ways, end of those post-War hopes, preparation for the next war. For it was followed by Hitler's advent to power in January 1933. I first met Adam von Trott, then a beautiful youth of nineteen, as a guest of Swinton. I said to him, 'Roll up the map of Europe': I understood Hitler's mentality well enough to know that he would never give up. And I knew Germany and German; through my intense friendship with Adam I had a window into the German mind and soul, if nothing else. I had recommended him for a Rhodes scholarship. With that he came up to Balliol. The rest of the tragic sequel came about in the years that followed.

The Rhodes group formed a distinct connection in College, friends from their experiences in South Africa, united by their devotion to Milner, his 'Kindergarten'. Milner was partly German by birth, more by education, a great administrator. Though an Imperialist, a rare bird in English politics, and regarded with horror by innocent Liberals as a reactionary, he was an independent spirit, not made on conventional lines, and ended up sympathetic to the Labour Party. I once asked Lionel Curtis what was the secret of Milner's hold on them all. He could not tell me, himself the 'Prophet' of the group.

I should here explain that there was a category of Fellows we called 'Fifty-Pounders'. These were original Prize Fellows who were specially attached to the College and whose Fellowships were renewed – partly to fill the gaps made by the War. The most powerful of the group was Geoffrey Dawson, since he had been estates bursar during an interval in his long editorship of the *Times*. Buckle had been editor for nearly thirty years, from 1884 to 1912; Dawson for another thirty, from 1912 to 1919, and from 1923 to 1942. No wonder the paper, at the heyday of its influence, was spoken of as the 'All Souls Parish Magazine'.

Dawson, born Robinson (and always known to his friends as 'Robin'), had to change his name on inheriting a maternal estate in Yorkshire. A devout Churchman, his personal affiliations were with Halifax and Lang, whom he could call Cosmo. He was a heavyweight, and a bit pompous. He was not popular with the junior Fellows; Archie Campbell, a man of principle, detested him. Oddly enough he was popular with me and would tease the innocent Leftist in a friendly way, which I responded to. He was an Etonian: would I have been a 'wet-bob' or a 'dry-bob'? Would I go to Ascot with him? He would be arrayed in grey tails, with grey topper – I would no more think of going to Ascot than of flying to the moon. He twice asked me to join his great newspaper – nor would I think of that: it would have killed me, as it killed McDowall. Naturally, I warmed to him, much more than to the academic Woodward.

Why did he single me out for notice among the junior Fellows? I thought it was because I was a Labour candidate. So he would tease me about my former revered leader, Ramsay MacDonald, and mock his pronunciation of his son's name, 'Mawcom'. When Arthur Henderson died, he told me that he had ended up, the old boiler-maker, distinctly 'warm' – he left over £30,000. He would take me for a walk round Magdalen, and tell me things about Curtis, that master in the art of wire-pulling, which few knew. Only he could write the artful Prophet's biography, he said.

Though he could write forcefully and wrote some historic leaders – 'Home Thoughts across the Seas', for instance, to reprove Baldwin's indolence and wake him up – one never thought of Dawson as a journalist. He had always been an editor, from editing an English paper in Johannesburg. In home politics he was far more powerful than any ordinary Cabinet minister, in constant touch with Neville Chamberlain and Halifax. He was the first person to tell us what was what about that deleterious couple, Edward VIII and Mrs Simpson. I was blissfully ignorant, and *wrong* – youthfully in favour of love having its way! Still more in hope of getting rid of Baldwin (as was Churchill).

But Dawson was totally ignorant of foreign affairs, his ignorance confirmed by a Barrington-Ward, brother of a Fellow who was dropped from College for boasting of his not serving in the War. How could they have been so wrong about Germany and the Germans, Hitler and his obvious intention, made perfectly clear in *Mein Kampf*, of reversing the verdict of Versailles and resuming the march to the domination of Europe? They didn't bother to read *Mein Kampf*, where the programme was laid out for all to read. They didn't know Germany or German, or Europe; they knew South Africa and the Empire. Then why didn't they recognise the threat to it?

I will not repeat what I wrote in *All Souls and Appeasement*. Dawson recognised only the threat from Italy in the Mediterranean. I kept up the argument with him: Italy is only a secondary threat, it is Germany that is the prime danger. The Foreign Office saw it well enough, and some unknown encouragement came from that quarter. The *Times* reflected the attitude of the City – which was pro-German and anti-French – and of the upper classes throughout the country. This was what kept me on the Left, nothing else – except that in those days the working classes did have a raw deal.

I was made to pay for sticking my neck out about Appeasement, which was as popular as it was short-sighted. Leo Amery said a disillusioning thing to me: in politics it was a mistake to walk too far ahead of people. Amery had a better anti-Appeasement record than any politician; he knew Central Europe and what the Germans were up to – and was kept out, as was Churchill. So there was nothing odd or eccentric about my line, based on the historic tradition of British policy through the centuries – as Chamberlain's ignorance was not. The best historian in these matters, Namier, and I were at one.

This is the place to say that there was no majority for Appeasement in the College, as people mistakenly suppose. The majority were against it: all the junior Fellows, except Quintin Hogg, who was caught as a Chamberlainite candidate. Among the seniors Grant Robertson was vehemently opposed to it; so was Arthur Salter; so was Reggie Coupland. In London Radcliffe, clever man, knew what nonsense it was, and carried young John Sparrow with him. Lord Brand, though one of the Milner-Rhodes group, opposed Appeasement: he knew Germany too well. Even Lionel Curtis never spoke a word in favour of it.

I fear now that the very title of my little memoir, *All*

Souls and Appeasement, gave people – since most people hardly read beyond a title and are certainly incapable of judging the contents – the idea that the College as such was associated with that fatally mistaken policy. This was not so. When the little book appeared it was attacked by a very junior Fellow, only just elected, young Wolfenden, who was able to instruct me that this 'was not the way to do it'. (That unpromising piece of mischief came to an early end in a bath in Moscow.) Headlam's reproof came to mind, administered to a young cleric in his diocese who attacked Bishop Barnes of Birmingham – he had the minimum of belief – for knowing no theology. Headlam told him off: 'It is true that the Bishop of Birmingham knows very little theology, *but it is not for you to say so.*'

Our chaplain Hutchinson was dining out one evening at Cambridge with Barnes, when chaplain of Trinity. Barnes, who was a wealthy man, paused between two coats hanging up, one a fur-coat, the other a tailored affair complete with astrakhan collar. Choosing the latter, he said, 'I think this is more befitting a humble minister of the Gospel.'

The College has a clear record on Appeasement. It happened that a few of its leading figures in the public eye were wrong: Halifax and Simon, Donald Somervell and, above all, Dawson. There was no concatenation among them, it was just an accident. Thank heaven that the little pipsqueak Sam Hoare – who went on defending it after the consequences had nearly destroyed our country – was not one of ours: he was a reject from an earlier examination. It would have been too much to have had him there too.

Dawson had been Milner's private secretary. Brand served in the South African civil service during the same period. He became a power in the City, managing director of Lazard's, a director of Lloyds, etc. We spoke with respect of his 'ice-cold financial intellect'. During the crisis of 1931 he said that there were only two people who understood the pros and cons of the Gold Standard – himself and Keynes – and they disagreed. He was not really a cold man, but reserved, though I heard him say that he had defeated Warden Adams in the Fellowship examination. So why should not I say that Roger Makins and I had defeated the impeccable John Hicks, the coming medievalists, K.B. McFarlane, W.A. Pantin *et al.*?

Lord Brand was a brother-in-law of the Astors and knew the banker Schacht well, who collaborated with Hitler and helped to finance Germany's rapid re-armament. But Brand was not talkative, was closed up in his private grief. His only son, a charming boy, was killed in the second War, and his wife died. Poor Bob carried around with him their photos in a little case which stood in his bedroom wherever he was. It is strange that his correct information about what was happening in Germany should have had no influence on his friends.

He once told me something fascinating. He was supposed to have been descended from a Lord Frederick Cavendish. Instead of that 'tenth transmitter of a foolish face', he was descended, in the irregular Regency way, from the eminent statesman, Lord Grey of the Reform Bill. At his fine place in Northamptonshire he showed me Grey's portrait – I saw at once how like him Brand was, the same high lofty brow, the noble cranium.

It is curious that we should not have realised that Amery was one of the most interesting of all the Fellows. There were reasons for this: in College he sat back and didn't say much. He was so hard at work in the outside world, and in various fields, that he regarded a week-end in College as a rest (as also did hard-pressed Lang). Amery has also been quite overlooked and underestimated in political life. Intrinsically he was a more interesting man than Simon, who was far more in the public eye. Since in College they were mates there is an example of the advice one could give the other in what Amery wrote to Simon at the latter's resignation over Conscription in 1916 (see above, p. 60). In other words he was saying that the vast Liberal victory of 1906 was a false dawn, the backwash of Gladstonian Liberalism. Many promising persons, with their careers and hopes, were stranded by the collapse – there was never to be a revival of the Liberal Party, in spite of the optimistic illusions of such as Keynes. Simon himself was stranded until he teamed up with the Tories behind the façade of a 'National' government in 1931.

Meanwhile Amery went ahead in various government posts, mainly concerned with the Empire and Commonwealth. As such he travelled all round the world; he may be said to have had a world-view, far more than most ordinary politicians. Simon, as we have seen, was a Gladstonian Little Englander, ignorant of the outside world, Amery more far-seeing. Even so, his hopes about Empire and Commonwealth were to be no less dashed.

Still, he accomplished a great amount of good work, especially in Africa, and much enjoyed himself, as we see from his two vivacious books of outdoor reminiscences, *Days of Fresh Air* and *In the Wind and the Rain*. (He was a better writer than speaker.) In July 1902 he wrote a long report of a trek into as yet unexplored Rhodesia, to W.P. Ker, of whom there was a devoted cult among the Fellows. (I just missed him, for he died on Monte Rosa the summer before my election, though I became even more an admirer of his work. We had a bust of him in the smoking-room to keep him in mind.)

Amery reported: 'There has been no such invasion of Southern Central Africa by All Souls as that by Robinson[1] and myself have just accomplished.' The duck they shot were described as 'swapping mallards', in the words of our Mallard Song. Dawson started his journalistic career on the Johannesburg *Star*. On a later tour of South Africa we

_____
[1] i.e. Dawson – see above, p.78.

find notes of what these young men of Milner's Kindergarten accomplished during their brief ascendancy. Lionel Curtis as town clerk made the blueprint for Johannesburg as a great city, parks, drainage system and all. He started municipal institutions all over the Transvaal, and next carried through the 'astonishing campaign' of propaganda and persuasion that led to the Union of South Africa. At one point Amery signalises Curtis's exceptional insight into government and its exigencies.

In 1907, a group of them celebrated an All Souls Gaudy in Johannesburg, 'super flumina Babylonis' – Amery, Dawson, Brand, Perry – as I have done, on my own, going through Wyoming, in California, or at home in Cornwall. It is a tribute to the group's activities that all the machinery started by them was taken over by the Afrikaners, Botha and Smuts, when they came into their own.

A rare pamphlet celebrated the group, *Government by Mallardry*. The *Times* itself, in those days, was, as I have noted, sometimes called derogatively the 'All Souls Parish Magazine'. In the Thirties no less than seven members of Council at Oxford were members of the College. All this, in the normal human way, led to much envy within the university and beyond. Even the all-powerful Hankey in Whitehall was on his guard against our influence – rather too liberal in his view.

Donald Somervell, who became Attorney General, was not a lawyer of the first rank like Simon or Wilfrid Greene, Radcliffe or Quintin Hogg. He was an agreeable man, not without charm, but a devout Appeaser, anti-Churchill. He considered Chamberlain's *démarche* at Munich 'a miracle of timing', according to Radcliffe, who regarded it with contempt – no Appeaser he, a first-class brain. After the second German war Churchill was given an historic reception in Westminster Hall by both parties. At lunch in buttery I said provocatively, 'The Chamberlainites must have turned in their graves.' Somervell fell for the bait, flushed hot in the face, and blurted that he wasn't in his grave. He went on to downgrade Churchill and give all the credit for re-armament to Lord Swinton.

The only thing of interest to me in Somervell was his father, who had taught young Winston at Harrow, and recognised his gift for writing essays. Self-willed as always, the boy wouldn't do classics or mathematics, but came up with pockets stuffed with what he had written. Donald Somervell had a peculiar background, he had taken a Science School and then law. He fancied himself as a conversationist; his luck ran out in 1945, when he lost both his seat and his wife.

Sir Dougal Malcolm, Dougie to us, was eminently clubbable, and as Lord Mallard in succession to Lang was a pillar of Common Room life, and sat long over the port. He emerged from his South African experience to become head of the Chartered South Africa Company. Cousin to half the Scottish aristocracy, he was eminently sociable and, a gifted linguist as well as Latin versifier, he was more European in his contacts. He never spoke up for Appeasement. Rich and kindly, he invited me to dine at his London house, introduced me to the son of F.S. Oliver, whose work on American Federalism had much influenced them intellectually. Curtis had hoped to federate the British Empire! No go. Dougie introduced me also to the grandeur of Powerscourt – now half burned out – when I went to Dublin in pursuit of Swift, whose biography I hoped to write.[2]

Perry was another of the group, who served in South Africa longer than any, so we saw little of him. The most remarkable of the group was Lionel Curtis, in a way their spiritual leader, for 'the Prophet' had a message, which went back to his Evangelical origins. Few know now how

[2] Hopes not fulfilled till forty years later when, in retirement freed from College research, I could turn more to my literary interests.

remarkable he was, and few there were to do justice to him. For, biographically, he had bad luck. His house at Kidlington burned down with all his historic papers. Dermot Morrah was supposed to write his biography but deviated into heraldry. The academic lady who came to me for information had two suitcases full of materials on him stolen from her car.

Curtis was essentially constructive, a constitution-maker, a kind of Abbé Sieyès, if he had known who he was. For India he was the inventor of 'Diarchy' – handing over government of the provinces largely to Indians while retaining control at the centre. He was concerned in the negotiations that led to the Anglo-Irish Treaty of 1922 and the creation of the Irish Free State (cf. the Orange Free State). He created Chatham House, the Royal Institute for International Affairs, the Oxford Preservation Trust, one loses count of it all.

He had the art of making anyone do what he wanted, keeping himself in the background, as if disinterested, wanting nothing for himself. He did it all off his own bat, having no money of his own, or any official position. T.E. Lawrence was his closest friend in College, and years after I succeeded to that position. Our relations became affectionate, though years apart.

I cannot write all I know about him, but from early on I watched his operations. He wanted me to write a scene for a church pageant at Kidlington; Alice Buchan was to write another. I was determined to do nothing of the sort and, very junior, didn't know that I could. So Arthur Salter's clerical brother was brought in from Kidlington to persuade me. I wrote my scene all right – and laughed at how I had been caught.

Curtis took me along with a small party to tea at Chequers – he had it in mind to corral Ramsay MacDonald for some purpose or other. It was the only time I set eyes on my sainted leader. He was the illegitimate son of a Scotch squire, and the part was natural to him (also the complex it gave rise to). Ramsay was an admirable host, showed us the pictures with pride. A man of taste, he was particularly fond of a Ferdinand Bol, pupil of Rembrandt. The wary Scot, whose hands were 'calloused with wire-pulling', according to philosopher McTaggart of Cambridge, was not coralled on this occasion. But Lionel never gave up – that was part of the art, and Geoffrey Dawson gave me instances of how it worked.

Once I witnessed a rather discreditable scene. One summer evening Lionel brought Mr ffenell – who was a Schumacher from South African days – to dine with a very few of us. Ffenell came down from his Wytham estate, for Lionel wanted him to leave it to the university. The Abbé Woodward, who liked to walk in the woods there, was in the chair. He proceeded to inveigh against rich men who made donations to the university in the hope of getting honorary degrees, etc. Inwardly I was appalled. The Abbé had not been above getting a Kahn grant to travel with his wife around the world. Lionel sat tight and said not a word – but he got the Wytham estate for the university.

He was a lifelong friend of Lionel Hitchens, the Cornish shipowner. These two handsome young fellows had met at evensong in New College Chapel as freshmen, evening light streaming through Reynolds's famous west window. 'It was love at first sight,' said Lionel. (One couldn't say such a thing today. A vanished – and more innocent – world!) Hitchens was killed in the second German war by a direct hit on Church House in Westminster. 'He went out in a chariot of fire,' said Lionel. There was a stoical element in this old Evangelical.

And, for all his being so 'square', he knew all the facts of life.[3] He told me something of the sex goings-on of the

---

[3] He said that in his day the Public Schools were 'sinks of iniquity – *perfect sinks of iniquity*'. I kept my smiles to myself, but relished the phrase.

Johannesburg gold-bugs, Barney Barnato and such – no space for all that he told me at one time and another – about the corrupt Valentine Chirol, Birkenhead accepting *douceurs*, perhaps he regarded them in the light of briefs – from the Indian Princes. One thinks of Chesterton's poem about the former F.E., a beguiling rogue, very far from 'impeccable'. Curtis was no reactionary. He knew Kipling well from South African days, and told me stories of him. He summed up Kipling as one part grouching reactionary, the other side inspired prophet. Kipling himself disapproved of Curtis for having 'sold the pass' – in India, and over Ireland.

A smoking-room scene makes me laugh still. Lord Faringdon was coming to see Lionel, in order to present a book to the Codrington.

Lionel: 'Why do I confuse Lord Faringdon and Lord Berners?' (Gerald Berners became my guest from time to time.)

Quintin Hailsham: 'Ask Leslie: he knows.'

Lionel, persisting loudly: 'But why should I confuse Lord Berners with Lord Faringdon?'

Quintin, naughtily: 'Ask Leslie: *he* knows.'

Lionel: 'Do you mean that he is an enemy of the family?'

I had never heard this blissful Victorian meiosis for it. At this the pantry-man came round the screen: 'Lord Faringdon to see you, sir.' Had he been behind the screen, and heard the exchange? The fact was that Gerald Berners lived at Faringdon, Gavin Faringdon not; he lived at splendid Buscot. A Labour peer, he invited me there, but I did not care for the company I was intended to fall for. Miss Susan Lawrence, first woman Cabinet Minister, used to stay. When her top civil servant went in for his first interview, he came out with, 'Perfect specimen of the *virago intacta*.'

3. The Thirties

Lionel was a grand raconteur, and had a comic story of our Craster, Bodley's Librarian. Craster came from an immensely old Northumbrian family, from Craster Tower, and originally had an apostrophe in his name, and as Margot Oxford put it, not 'a roof nor a rafter' to his mouth. He was also of an old-fashioned courtesy, which added point to what happened when a party of guests came to be shown round the Bodleian. Craster didn't know, but among them was an ex-official who had been sacked from the Foreign Office for dealing in French currency. He made the mistake of asking how Sir Thomas Bodley had made all his money. Craster replied as if knowingly, 'Ah – he was in the diplomatic service.'

Curtis thought that a statue should be erected to Mrs Simpson for getting rid of Edward VIII – all that one wanted from royal personages was that they should be punctual, and Edward was always late. Craster, an Edwardian addict of puns: 'So he became the – Ah! – *late* King.' Why subscribe to the conventional objection to puns? They have an authentic ancestry going right back to Shakespeare, if not to Chaucer.

No one now will be able to get the true quality, the inwardness, of Lionel Curtis to account for the influence he exerted on other remarkable men in his time. Geoffrey Dawson told me, as I have said, that only he could write Lionel's biography. He proceeded to describe the Curtis technique of pressuring Prime Ministers into awarding honours in return for public service. The essence of it was – Never give up – and Dawson cited examples. Another clue was that he wanted nothing for himself, and operated keeping religiously in the background. To myself I registered that his disinterestedness amounted to complete interestedness.

Remarkably, too, he had imagination, where others had not. When younger, this politician had written verse, which he confided to me – surprisingly, it was rather good. It was thus understandable that he was the only Fellow who had T.E. Lawrence's confidence, and understood the complexities of that self-tortured mind. So too he was the only one who understood my own Manichean cult of illness – I held that it sharpened the edge of one's brain. Heaven knows I endured enough periodic pain without cultivating it!

✳

What amusing exchanges one was present at in those days! Sir William Holdsworth, not having been elected a Prize Fellow, became a Professorial Fellow later. Immensely learned in law, he was yet a shy man and an innocent. Once naughty John Foster, always out to shock the bourgeois, was explaining to Holdsworth what Lesbianism was: I saw a blush creep up the back of his neck under the white hairs.

He had no social sense. One evening, when he was in the chair at dinner, a foreign guest was placed on his right. Holdsworth, who had no languages, said not a word. Eventually the guest, who may have heard about the Bible Clerks, thought that perhaps he was expected to speak first. So he said, 'Have you any undergraduates?'

Holdsworth took a shy look at him, and said, 'None.'

This non-plussed the foreigner, who thought for a bit, and then said: 'How is she then?'

To this, Sir William: 'How is who?'

The foreigner, further mystified: 'The nun.'

Holdsworth, who may have thought there was some aspersion on the College, said crossly: 'I never said anything about a nun.'

The foreign guest repeated what he had heard. Somebody had to explain the vagaries of the English language, and the difference between 'None' and 'Nun'. It was more than poor Holdsworth could take. He got up quickly and left the room. Young Isaiah Berlin was of course convulsed. 'Entertainments we have assisted at' – I had better get on to something more serious.

❖

The College connection with India was historically remarkable. Three Viceroys! Of these Curzon did a fine job in preserving the splendid monuments of the Indian past, which fascinated him. (Do Indians remember him for it?) And we now know that in the row with Kitchener which ended his Viceroyalty Curzon was in the right – as President Truman was against General MacArthur: civilian rule must have ultimate authority over military. Then again at Lausanne Curzon saved this country from a war with Turkey after the hubristic Greek advance into Asia minor, with its nemesis. He was miserable at not becoming Prime Minister instead of Baldwin; he could not have done worse for the country's interests – at least he understood Europe.

Curzon had a typical quarrel with the College. He wanted to put coloured glass in the great end-windows of the Codrington, himself as Chancellor of the university in the centre, with a purple ribbon along the range to connect up. This would have ruined the beautiful clear light of the Georgian glass. It was lost by only one vote, that of the admirable W.P. Ker, and for long Curzon did not forgive us.

The Georgian Hall of Hawksmoor the Edwardians had similarly spoiled with their heavy stained glass, College worthies, with armorial bearings. In the second War we took the opportunity to put it away for safety and never put it back. There were several other encumbrances, like the huge Speaker's chair from the old House of Commons, which had been Speaker Abbott's, a Fellow.

Before becoming Viceroy Chelmsford had been Governor of Queensland (a Victorian Herbert from All Souls had been Prime Minister there and for long Secretary for the Colonies), and then of New South Wales. As Viceroy of

India he advanced a stage further towards self-government, with the Montagu-Chelmsford Reforms. To help MacDonald form a minority government in 1924 Chelmsford took over the Admiralty. He was not a party man, but a servant of the state.

It is generally held that Halifax's rule in India formed the best part of his long career. His religiosity enabled him to understand Gandhi, and he advanced self-government to its penultimate stage. He also did a good job as Ambassador to Washington, to which Churchill relegated him, to get him out of the Foreign Office. There is no defence for his coming to the rescue of Neville Chamberlain with his fatal trust in Hitler, or their willingness to come to terms with the gangsters in Germany. Halifax was too superior, and perhaps too Christian, to understand such lower mortals. Hugh Cecil put it theologically, 'Edward does not believe in Original Sin.' It is said that he never read *Mein Kampf* until the Queen (now Queen Mother) lent him her copy.

One thing amuses me: when he went to the footstool at Berchtesgaden and was met by the divine Führer, Halifax from his immense height was only just forestalled from handing Hitler his overcoat, thinking him a footman. A defect they all had in handling the gangsters was their British self-complacency, their superiority-complex. Coming back from hobnobbing with the criminal Göring, who had master-minded the murder-campaign of June 30, 1934, and asked what he thought of Göring, Halifax said that he looked like 'a head gamekeeper at Chatsworth'. True, they had hunted together. When asked what Molotov was like, I heard him say: 'Like a buttoned-up secondary schoolmaster.' Ernest Bevin was better at dealing with such types: he regarded Molotov as a murderer; Molotov complained that our Ernest was not a gentleman.

Perhaps Halifax was bored with mere politics; he much preferred hunting in Yorkshire and invited me to stay at

Garrowby. (I could not have borne daily chapel.) He had his private tragedy from the second War – he had served in the first. One son was killed, another had both legs smashed by a falling bomb, which did not explode or he too would have been killed.

Both Oman and Robertson had Anglo-Indian backgrounds. Sir Thomas Raleigh, another Scot, was the legal member of the Viceroy's Council. Sir Maurice Gwyer, Chief Justice of India, on his retirement became Vice-Chancellor of a large university, general promoter of education. Rushbrook Williams was chief secretary and foreign minister to the Maharajah of Patiala, then of Nowanagur. Back at home Sir Ernest Trevelyan was Reader in Indian Law. F.W. Bain spent his life in India as professor in the Deccan College at Poonah. He was deeply interested in Indian mythology and legend, and wrote a series of books, of which *Digits of the Moon* had some renown in its time. But he made no money, and retiring on a small pension lived poorly in obscurity in London and never came to College.

Simon headed the famous Commission which investigated the whole problem of the government and future constitution of India. It might have brought off something, given half a chance: Simon was deeply hurt by his frustration, but as usual kept his lips shut. Leo Amery was Secretary of State for India, under his Old Harrovian friend Churchill, and was by no means so right-wing or opposed to advance as people thought. My particular friend, Penderel Moon, devoted his life, and his remarkable brain-power to India. Out there he came to sympathise with Congress and realised that the British meant to hand over at some point. Premature, with the sharpest of minds, he was asked to resign. When he came back I got him to write the volume in my series, *Men and their Times*, on Warren Hastings – distinguished for seeing the great pro-consul from the Indian point of view, as against Macaulay's juvenile Whig prejudice.

At the take-over Moon was summoned back to India by Nehru, and had an appalling assignment at Partition, on the border between India and Pakistan – as laid down by Radcliffe. Hundreds of thousands of Muslims were fleeing west, Hindus fleeing east – and massacring each other comparably. Moon could have made a fortune like Clive's. Instead he organised trains and transport, saved thousands of lives, and came to be regarded as a guru. He then went on to preside over the economic development of India for Nehru, whom he admired – and he had a positive weakness for Gandhi. In his retirement, as I have noted, he wrote a splendid book on the whole extraordinary epic of British rule in India, treating it from the original perspective of Anglo-Indian co-operation. There is no doubt that Moon – like so many of the old ICS – loved India, and I have no doubt that he had greatness of soul.

An Indian eminence came to live with us for some years in College. This was Radakrishnan, as Professor of Eastern Philosophy and Religion. With us, his special friend was G.D.H. Cole, on the Left. A strict Brahmin, Rada enjoyed a special diet, and the servants were somewhat taken aback by his ritual ablutions. At Gandhi's assassination he went into strict mourning, several days' seclusion. Since he became the first President of India we have a full-length portrait of him on the dais in Hall, with the other grandees, Curzon, Halifax and the great Lord Salisbury.

We did not know that this holy man was a devout womaniser. I learn that he gave a lecture on the ideal of fidelity in marriage – with a mistress in the front row of the audience. He was an idealist: I thought him a humbug. He was Vice-Chancellor of an Indian university, with salary, on leave to be Professor of Eastern Philosophy and Religion at Oxford with full salary; from which he was on leave to be Indian Ambassador in Moscow no doubt with salary plus expenses. What did he do with it all? I was friendly enough with him, and he gave me his high-minded tract comparing

Jesus Christ with the Buddha. It was more gratifying to hear from him that Kipling's *Kim* was the best Western book on India – as against the humbug of Lionel Trilling, over-estimating E.M. Forster's *Passage to India*, as all liberals do. In fact Indians find Forster's book patronising. We never saw Forster at All Souls, though we gave hospitality to the Left-wing Trilling. I did not think highly of his *Matthew Arnold*, which ignored the clue to Arnold's personality (his Celtic ancestry) and his crucial life's work for education. Nor should I have welcomed the author of the appalling *Sprichwort* for which Forster has been given credit by the unthinking: 'If I had to choose between betraying my friends and betraying my country, I hope I should have the guts to betray my country.'

That piece of humbug is all too facile, since the English are so easy-going, but it had a fatal influence on his faithful Cambridge following. Of these I set eyes on Guy Burgess only once, when Goronwy Rees brought him in for a drink after dinner. Burgess was in the smoking-room only half-an-hour before the junior Fellow came up to complain to me – I was senior that night – that Burgess had made a pass at him. What was I supposed to do about that? I said merely: 'Well, you can keep out of his way.' Goronwy was Burgess's closest friend, but – whatever we may think of his irresponsibility – Rees was neither a Communist nor a spy (but did he, or did he not, know that Burgess was the latter?)

It is significant that, among our Fellows in the Foreign Office, the most silent and reclusive (he later became an ambassador) was the only one who suspected the criminal Philby. This offers a contrast with the more publicising members of MI5 whose business it was but who had no suspicion.

✤

Ordinary normal married professors had their houses out in Oxford, so we permanent residents saw little of them, unless some intermission in domestic bliss brought them into College for a change. One such brought in the Professor of Civil Law, Francis de Zulueta. Though a naturalised Englishman who had lived all his life in this country, he confessed that he did not understand the English and their ways of thought. A big, burly handsome Basque, he was not only an ardent Catholic but an ultramontane, a real reactionary – not friendly to Anglicans, unlike my friend Gervase Mathew, a Dominican who was constantly in and out of All Souls, or bringing his brother David, the archbishop, to dine with me.

At dinner, when Zulueta headed the table as senior, he was reluctant to say the grace to a crew of heretics. After a bit he found that we were not so bad after all. He allowed that, since I was in a state of 'invincible ignorance', I should be more lightly judged in the hereafter than he would be. Wasn't his faith then rather disadvantageous to him, I inquired. He had no answer to that one.

He was a cousin of Cardinal Merry del Val, the reactionary Papal Secretary of State to the simple Pius X, who condemned Modernism in all its forms. Zulu's cousin ruled in the Vatican, pulled all the strings, during that reign. But he did not become Pope: his liberal-minded rival succeeded as Benedict XV. Zulu was candid enough to tell me that Merry del Val was thought too friendly with the youth of Trastevere. He died under an operation, having swallowed his false teeth – or so it was said.

Zulueta was an expert Latinist. But so was Professor R.W. Lee, who wrote a set of verses on the accession of Pius XI, the librarian who had read in the Bodleian. Lee, the high and dry Rationalist, received a Papal medal – which did not give unadulterated pleasure to the devout Zulu – so devout that, privately, he was a Franciscan tertiary, and was buried as such. No less privately, I thought his thinking mere prejudice. However, even so, it gave one a useful insight into the intolerant fanatical Spanish mentality. Naturally, during the Spanish Civil War, he was ardently pro-Franco. That shocking affair was less acutely divisive among us than the more critical and dangerous Appeasement of Hitler became.

Simon provided a curious case, for, though he loved the College, nobody loved him. Junior lawyers, like ribald John Foster, had a habit of telling stories about Simon's faulty personal touch. Simon himself put it down to shyness in his Memoirs, which he gave me, '*amicus amico*'. I had no reason to complain of his reticence, he would tell me things few would – even of the social mishaps to which he was prone. When he was young he had been bidden to dine with the redoubtable Cornish Radical and pro-Boer Leonard Courtney. Simon and wife duly arrayed themselves and arrived at a house where they were clearly not expected, that of W.L. Courtney, Editor of the *Fortnightly Review*.

As a legal member of Asquith's government Simon had been summoned to Balmoral when George V had to resort to the lawcourts to quash the libel that he had been married as a young naval officer in Malta. Queen Mary took Simon out on the gravel, punctuating her declaration with her parasol: 'George has many faults, but not *that one!*'

Naturally, I had no love for the façade of a 'National' government. But it was reasonable for the conservative section of Liberals to line up with the Conservatives; the Radical section should have joined up with Labour – as I was always urging upon Keynes – and end the farce of a separate Liberal Party. As a Labour candidate I was committed to the ridiculous proposition of 'nationalisation' of almost everything. Simon said to me peaceably that the competition of the four great railway systems was all to the good. I recognised that he was right. And were we not proud of the old Great Western throughout the West

Country? He had bad luck in being Foreign Secretary in the early Thirties: he may not have been so bad as people made out. Over the Japanese invasion of Manchuria, for instance, what could we have done? That was America's pigeon, and Simon told me that the Americans were not going to move. Over Hitler and Germany Vansittart and the Foreign Office were of course right. Simon told me that he often had to defend Vansittart in Cabinet. Van spoiled himself by writing his advice in the style of the Edwardian *littérateur* he fancied himself to be, as anyone can see from reading his autobiography, *The Mist Procession*. (Silly title; why didn't somebody tell him?)

Vansittart was kicked upstairs by Neville Chamberlain, who put Cadogan in his place. Then Cadogan saw how things really were: 'It has all worked out as Van said it would, *and I never believed it.*' Fancy Chamberlain following the advice of a Horace Wilson, who knew nothing whatever of Germany and Europe, and told him what he wanted to hear. Chamberlain said to Kenneth Clark: 'He is the most remarkable man in England, I could not get on for a day without him.' An able junior Fellow, Con O'Neill, knew Germany and protested against the mistaken course they were following. He was carpeted by the egregious Wilson, who told him that a civil servant had no business to concern himself with policy. What about himself, so wrong?

Once when Simon was lunching in buttery and saying What *should* he do? his old pal Robertson shouted across, 'Resign!' Simon was never going to do that again. He had done it in 1916 over Conscription – where the young Nonconformist was ignorantly wrong – and lost his footing in politics for the next decade and a half.

Simon and Amery, as we have seen, had been elected together. No one noticed Amery much. He was the most underestimated of the political figures of his time. His was a curious case, hard to account for – today he is the most forgotten of them all, though more worth remembering. It is partly that he was a modest man – a defect in a politician. Then, too, he was independent-minded. We juniors thought of him as a reactionary, and yet that was not correct either. He was one of Milner's Young Men and had been through the South African War as a war-correspondent, like his fellow-Harrovian Churchill. He wrote the *Times* History of the War in several volumes. Yet he hardly seemed to operate as one of the group; a dedicated Imperialist with a vision all his own, he did any amount of good work for Africa, Australia, New Zealand, Canada – and got no credit for it at home.

I do not remember him ever once speaking up at a College meeting, unlike Simon, or holding forth in the smoking-room. He seemed content to take a back seat. It used to please me that my Leftist friend G.D.H. Cole and he always got on well together.

It was a pity that Amery was not more powerful in politics, for he was a man of action – and Baldwin, as leader of his party and the key-man in politics in the inter-war years, was disinclined for that. Unlike the rest of them Amery knew Europe well, and was anti-Appeasement. He had had an early interview with Hitler, in which the Führer played him his pacifist gramophone-record. Amery was not taken in, as the Appeasers were. They managed to keep him out, as they kept out Churchill and Lloyd George, men of action who meant business. Amery understood too well how things were. 'I sensed an undercurrent of mutual sympathy, based on a common shrinking from definite policies and decisions, drawing MacDonald and Baldwin together.' He well understood what a fraud the 'National' government of 1931 was: 'the worst possible coalition of old gangs, including even the defunct Liberal Party.'

It included Simon, never a man of action, but who knew how defunct the Liberal Party was. Simon and Amery were like Box and Cox, when one was in the other was out. Simon had been in Asquith's government up to 1916, while

Amery as a Conservative was out. In the Conservative governments of the 1920s Amery was First Lord of the Admiralty – he knew a great deal about Defence (he was a brave man, a plucky fighter) – then Secretary of State for the Colonies, where he did a fine job. In 1940, when the disaster he had foreseen came about, Churchill made him Secretary of State for India, a post in which he was far from reactionary. In that *annus terribilis* he made a remark which astonished me: it revealed a conviction that *he* could have led the country out of disaster. He had all the courage necessary, and a less adventurous judgment than Churchill's. Of course politicians have to have a belief in themselves, or they wouldn't survive. But he had not Winston's genius, or the inspiration that upheld people in that hour of defeat, expressed in Churchill's magic words.

❖

One gets an insight into what people were thinking in College from the Betting Book. This went back to 1815, and where was Napoleon after Waterloo? – he might have got, the gambler, to the United States, as a brother had done. 'January 9, 1933: Hudson bets Rowse half-a-crown that Trotsky will return to place in the USSR within one year from today.' He never did: why did Geoffrey think that he would? 'December 16, 1933. MacGregor bets Pares £1 that Adolf Hitler will be given an honorary degree of this university within his [MacGregor's] tenure of the Drummond chair.'

This university? MacGregor was a Cambridge man, a bright spark, President of the Cambridge Union, Fellow of Trinity. (At one time we had no less than six former Fellows of Trinity.) But he had been blown up on the Menin Road during the war, and something went out of him. One would see him occasionally muttering away to himself. At the time of the financial crisis of 1931 he was dumbfounded, brought up in the purest Marshall tradition at Cambridge. Like the whole herd of academic economists he did not know what to think, except for Keynes, who was right, and Lionel Robbins, too dogmatically wrong.

'February 9, 1934. Hudson bets Rowse half-a-crown that the two Great Powers will be at war by Midsummer Day of this year.' They were not for a few 'locust' years yet. The same day: 'Berlin bets Rowse that, in the event of a war breaking out before June 1939 between Russia and Japan in which Japan is victorious, Trotsky if alive will return to power. 2/6 at stake. Settlement – none recorded.' 'August 11, 1934. Woodward bets Rowse and Jones [A.H.M. – historian of the Roman Empire] 1/– each that A. Hitler is not President, Chancellor, Vice-Chancellor, or under any other title Head, of the German Reich on the day of Encaenia 1935.' Woodward had a supercilious view of Hitler, and discounted him all through the Thirties. Encaenia was the degree ceremony in the Sheldonian, after which we gave a prodigious luncheon in the Codrington. A splendid spectacle, all the doctors in scarlet, tables the whole length of the great Library, the College silver displayed, fruit, flowers, ladies in their finery. Woodward, as domestic bursar, was always trying to abolish it.

'June 8, 1934. Austin [J.L., philosopher] bets Salter 4 to 1 in shillings that Mussolini is still in control of Italy on 25-VI-1936.' Of course the miscreant was. Our eminent international civil servant, a Liberal, was betting in accordance with his wishes. It is usually a mistake to think just as one would *like* things to be – as is notorious with people's views of Shakespeare. Yet people usually do, for, strictly speaking, they do not know how to think, though Salter did.

'May 11, 1935. Jay [Douglas] bets Berlin £1.2.6d at three to one that Dr Kurt Schuschnigg will no longer be Chancellor of Australia [*sic* for Austria] on Encaenia Day,

1936.' This bet was scribbled over and its terms altered – were they tight? 'May 13, 1935. Pares bets Oman three to one in shillings that Hitler will declare himself to be divine before Mussolini does so. [The chaplain to decide.]' I see Richard's point. I regularly called Hitler 'the divine Führer', many Germans thought of him as such. 'May 17, 1936. Faber bets Rowse 2-1 in half-crowns that Great Britain will be involved in a war with Italy within 5 years from this date.' Faber gave himself plenty of room here, and turned out to be right. 'May 16, 1937. Woodward bets Rowse 2/6d that within five years from the date of this bet there will be, or have been, a Russo-German rapprochement.' There was, and I paid up.

Warden Pember's time was running out, but it never occurred to me, unsophisticated as I was, that he would leave us. Before he retired he fulfilled his duty by taking on the Vice-Chancellorship according to the rota laid down by Laud, greatest of our Chancellors. As Archbishop, Laud was also our Visitor; as such, he imposed upon a reluctant College one of its most distinguished members: Jeremy Taylor. Always unpopular, Laud was usually right. Warden Pember put forward his friend Asquith for Chancellor. The Tories would not have it, and voted in the second-rate Lord Cave. Asquith, then Lord Oxford, said agreeably that some people would not vote for him because he was a bachelor – he had never taken the trouble to become M.A. – others because he wasn't a bachelor. (Margot!)

Pember upheld the dignity of the office, and of All Souls, but he had little sense of time – College meetings under him went on and on. Similarly with John Sparrow later – when I copied Lang's habit under Pember. The Archbishop sat at the top table on the dais in Hall, writing away at his letters. The pile grew higher and higher. If anything came up that concerned the Church, he rose, said his piece as briefly as possible, then back to his letters. I don't know how university business proceeded with Pember translating pounds, shillings and pence into Latin as he went.

One day Pares, contemplating Sparrow as Warden, whom he had not favoured, asked why it was that the combination of classics with the law meant negativeness. I will not say nullity, but neither Pember nor Sparrow had any constructive ideas – John confessed as much to me later. I had been keen on his election as Fellow, my junior by a few years. He had already made a reputation for himself as a schoolboy, editing the Poems of Henry King. He would make a recruit to literature. Why then did he not get on with it? He had a strain of perverseness by which he frustrated himself – and would others. Early on he had a fixation on the boring Dr Parr, 'the Whig Dr Johnson', collected his unreadable *Works*, and could talk of him *ad lib* if encouraged. Sparrow's mother, worried by it, said to me one day, 'Mr Rowse, can you do nothing about it?' What could I do about it? – John would take nothing from me. He also collected the most wearisome of all Cornish writers, the Reverend Richard Polwhele.

In Oxford John made a cult of fuddy-duddies. I went down to the Probationer's room below me to see how our young recruit was settling in. There he was, trilby hat on, a scarf wound tight about his neck, walking stick in hand, going round and round his table. What on earth was he doing, I asked. 'Trying to see what it feels like to be Garrod,'[4] said he. He also had a cult of another clever ass, Farquharson of University College. Brought to dine and placed at Warden Adams's right hand, he would turn round with a grimace, and 'What have I done to deserve this?' Then there was Geoffrey Madan, who had been Captain of

[4] H.W. Garrod, Senior Fellow at Merton.

the School at Eton, handsome as Apollo, with whom A.C. Benson was smitten. Madan was a brilliant classical scholar who had sat for the Fellowship examination but not made it. He had done absolutely nothing with his life, except marry a rich woman. John would bring him down, to eat our rations during the war. Frugal Robertson, who had come back to be domestic bursar, wouldn't stand for it and gave Madan a frosty reception. Nothing daunted, Madan gave us a silver snuff-box with the inscription, *tamen grato animo* (i.e. nevertheless). It was the sort of joke they liked. I used to call them John's 'Old Sillies', took no notice and went on with my work.

John did not get on with his. He was to write a Life of John Donne, and made a priceless collection of his early editions. But one Bald, whom I knew at the Huntington Library, a dull scholar, wrote the book. Then John was to do *the* edition of Pope. He had a fine eighteenth-century collection, but somebody else did the work.

In early years our relations were not so friendly as they should have been with our common literary interests. It is not unfair to say that he was jealous of my writing, and would say 'I admire your writing so *much*' – as if that was lost on me or had the slightest effect. He was encouraged in this by his friend Harold Nicolson, through whom so many young men had got a leg-up in literary life. John placed him beside me at dinner in Hall, having told him how keen I was on the poetry of Rilke. Uncle Harold – I was a friend of a nephew and kind to a son of his – took the opportunity to suggest that Rilke was a repressed homo. I had no sense at all, but recognised a pass, turned my back, and didn't address another word to him. If I had had more sense, and been a bit more complaisant – but I hadn't been at a Public School – I might have had a successful literary career, like the others.

Time had gone, and just before I reached the end of my first seven-year term, Warden Pember left the Lodgings for

3. The Thirties

Broncroft Castle. I could not accustom myself to the idea of the Lodgings without him. Springtime for me in College was over.

CHAPTER 4

Warden Adams

Warden Pember was succeeded by Lord Chelmsford. I remember nothing about an election, it was just taken for granted. But a new broom was evident. At College meeting the tables were brought up close to the dais, so that we could all attend to business, which was got through expeditiously. In the Lodgings the rich red Morris wall-paper of the dining room made way for apple-green. The drawing room was opened out to include the ante-room, a larger space for the crowded quarterly parties of Fellows. I did not often attend those.

And made no contact with the distant Vice-regal figure we rarely saw. I recall only one significant exchange with him. One day I asked him if he had ever gone back to India. 'No – if one was accustomed to travelling everywhere by special train it would be awkward to go about by ordinary ones.' An innocent question – for of course ex-Viceroys never returned to the scenes of their former grandeur. However, Lady Chelmsford was friendly, and I used to lend books to her daughter, who had literary interests and a pretty little room of her own beside the fine staircase in that Queen Anne house which Dr Clarke, the connoisseur, had built.

Then suddenly Warden Chelmsford died, in the garden out at Ginge watching cricket. This was the house of Rowland Prothero, who had a variegated career, and whom I saw only once, at breakfast. He was a literary figure, who had edited the *Nineteenth Century*, then the *Quarterly*; the Letters of Gibbon and then those of Byron. He had an intimate knowledge of farming, in France as well as England, and wrote a best-seller, *English Farming, Past and Present*, then another, *The Psalms in Human Life*. Becoming the administrator of the vast Bedford estates (then!), he set a model of agricultural improvement, housing for the workers, etc. In the 1914-18 war he did a grand job as Minister of Agriculture by increasing wheat production, when the country was nearly starved out by the German submarine campaign. He set up an Agricultural Wages Board to improve the wages and conditions of farm workers. All this good work under Lloyd George, which helped largely to win the war, was allowed to lapse by the paralytic do-nothing Toryism of Bonar Law and Baldwin. Prothero retired as Lord Ernle. His father had been rector of Whittingham, the parish in which was Queen Victoria's Osborne House in the Isle of Wight. Prothero began his career as a boy aiming a stone at the Prince Consort's backside going into church. After that he never looked back. He was one of those old Fellows whom I would most like to have known.

Caught by the emergency, whom were we to elect as Warden? W.G.S. Adams happened to be Sub-Warden, and made an obvious choice. Pares and I were banded together in everything, but here we were divided. Richard was an academic of the purest water. Here he agreed with Woodward. They were both against the London Fellows, the public figures, and wanted to make the College more academic. I thought this small-minded. The whole point of All Souls was in its uniqueness, as a bridge between the university and public life, good for both.

Why this small-mindedness? Partly inferiority-complex. They had the middle-class inferiority-complex against the upper-classes. Woodward once said to me early on that the gentry formed the worst stratum in society. Taken aback, I said but surely they were the people who had formed the countryside, planted the woods and parks, had a responsible attitude towards country life, etc. Woodward and Pares were suburbanites: I was a countryman.

Richard was the son of a professor, Sir Bernard Pares, but he was disapproved of for having the popular touch, and his books were readable. Father and mother lived apart, for Sir Bernard was really in love with Russia, on which he was an intimate authority, had known many of the leading figures, Kerensky, Miliukov, and the Imperial family. Sir Bernard's life had been broken in two by the Bolshevik Revolution, and we can see now what a tragic aberration that was. How much happier Russia would have been if it had never taken place, and Russia's evolution had proceeded more normally and constitutionally, as Sir Bernard and his Russian friends had hoped. They were defeated men. The senior Pares had been at Harrow with Pember, and occasionally came down to stay. I saw his fascination – so did Richard, and disapproved. He had reacted against his father, and this influenced his writing. He wrote an enormous research work on War and Trade in the West Indies. It was unreadable. At one point it became readable, with a brief sketch of an important Trelawny governor of Jamaica, and at once it was switched off. I asked Richard why. 'Oh, it wasn't history.' The academic fashion was then all against biography, the personal in history. But what was it about, if not about human beings? Richard took no notice: he was my senior, he knew better – and went on being unreadable. It was paradoxical, for as a human being he was scintillating. I understood the psychological root of the perverseness that frustrated him as a writer. He would learn nothing from me.

For Warden he was determined on a blameless academic. I was in favour of Adams, not much of an academic, but experienced in public life. He had been secretary to the wise Sir Horace Plunket, who promoted agricultural co-operation as the most hopeful way forward for Ireland, instead of murderous politicising. The political fanatics burned down his house for him. During the war Adams headed Lloyd George's private secretariat in the garden of 10 Downing Street. After the Irish Treaty it was said that he produced the most hopeful proposals ever put forward for the solution of the Ulster problem. An uncommunicative man, the most selfless and disinterested, he never said a word about it, or repined.

His heart was in agriculture. On Boar's Hill he kept pigs – he had a rotund, porcine figure himself. He experimented by letting the pigs feed themselves by rootling in a potato field. G.N. Clark said that the locals called him 'Starve-hog Adams'. In the university he promoted the School of Agriculture, and all over the nation he worked hard for the Young Farmers' Union, which he had fostered. He had no time to waste on political theory. Later on, after Salter's time, Warden Adams, no Party man, recruited Left-wing G.D.H. Cole to profess it.

He made a good Warden, and was moreover a dear man, apt to be right. He tried to capture the Regius Chair of Medicine for us; with our sights on 'social sciences' – God save the mark – we wouldn't have it. He was all for Alan Bullock for Prize Fellow. The mimic Isaiah could mock the Warden:[1] 'Bullock – Bullock. He's the man: he's got *it*.' I dare say he had, but we opted for someone less of a heavy-weight.

In Dublin Adams had married a wife from one of the old families. Muriel was a cousin of the famous art-collector, Sir Hugh Lane (drowned on the torpedoed *Lusitania*), and of all the Gwynnes – so we used to see the writer Stephen Gwynne. When I was pursuing Swift in Dublin Mrs Adams gave me an introduction to the grand Fitzgibbons and others. With her the Lodgings were not stylish, but homely;

---

[1] So could John Sparrow in the *Spectator*, as 'Professor Gladstone'.

she was shy, but sweet. And so kind. When I had a bad duodenal haemorrhage during the second War, and another month in the Acland, she made me a belly-band to hold up my deleterious stomach.

As for Richard Pares and me, sharp G.N. Clark spotted the difference between us. Though I was the fanatic, in theory, Richard was really the doctrinaire; when it came to action I was the compromiser. Nobody else spotted that. For I carried him and Geoffrey Hudson off to Douglas Cole's sessions of his new SSIP – Society for Socialist Inquiry and Propaganda – an up-dated Fabian group at Easton Lodge in Essex. This was the home of the famous Lady Warwick, former mistress of Edward VII. Richard was amused that I fell for this romantic relic, violet eyes and large expanse of bosom, pneumatic bliss. I had given her a book I later missed, François Mauriac's *La Province* – I read everything he wrote. Richard found a second-hand book, an unsuitable (or suitable) French novel by Paul de Kock, inscribed 'For lovely Warwick, from Albert Edward', some Christmas in the 1890s.

More seriously, I was teaching as hard as ever, now on a regular basis for Merton, who made me a member of their Common Room. There Garrod, who was the soul of it, was markedly kind, though I never wasted time attending his evening at-homes, as John Sparrow did. The most memorable of my pupils was a rich American, who was sophisticatedly amused by my attempts to marry conventional political theory with Marxism. This was indeed the axis of my lectures in the Old Library, and I found it a struggle to square the circle. Worry, worry – I still have an anxiety dream that I have to lecture and haven't had time to prepare it. The lectures were well attended, Ken Wheare in the audience, who later made a fine Professor of Political Institutions for us.

I was deputising for Salter, who became a good friend. He had not been welcomed by Pares and Berlin when he came to live in College, and he resented the treatment of those superior young intellectuals. When I came back I took a different line. His experience had made him far more interesting. He had begun, with Beveridge, as a civil servant pushing forward Lloyd George's social insurance campaign. In the war he had done a first-class job as director of Allied Shipping Control, and putting the convoy-system across the reluctant Admiralty, which ultimately defeated the submarines. He then moved to Geneva, to inaugurate the International Labour Office, in which Harold Butler, another Fellow, served.

Again I anticipate. What about College research?

Here I owed a debt to Pares. He was already familiar with the Public Record Office and London life. I did not know the ropes. He took me under his wing. We each had a room in No 1, Brunswick Square – subsequently obliterated by a direct hit in the Blitz, and Jane Austen's beautiful Square ruined. Together we would set out after breakfast for the Public Record Office and work there at our documents all day till 5 p.m., with only a biscuit or a bar of chocolate for lunch. We then walked up to the Institute of Historical Research for tea, more work till 8 p.m., when we went out to dine in Soho. Little did I realise that this was the worst regimen possible for a duodenal, and I got worse and worse.

To make ends meet in London, I dropped my Merton teaching for a temporary lectureship to evening students at the London School of Economics. Those evenings I walked the short distance through Lincoln's Inn Fields to Aldwych, a good tea in the Common Room at LSE, and my dreary lectures. I was not on the permanent staff there, and the institution had no allure for me. Sharing a room! I was in touch with some of the Faculty, friendly H.L. Beales, familiar Harold Laski, enchanting Eileen Power. Even the redoubtable Mrs Mair, Beveridge's Egeria, whom everybody disliked, became a friend. There was a cult of R.H.

Tawney, too noble for words: no doubt he was a good and great man, but – Rugby and Balliol – he had gone to the good. I could not aspire to such ethical altitudes, and never made the grade with him. Nor did I care for Lionel Robbins bombinating away. I liked quiet Morris Ginsberg, and actually found his sociology books useful for my lectures.

It was the students who depressed me. Their essays! They couldn't write English, the only one who could was a Lebanese. They had never even heard of Hazlitt. To what point their 'education'? No doubt mine were not fair specimens, merely evening classes, irregulars like me. I did not belong; it was just a convenient combination with the day's real work at the PRO. And I usually went back to All Souls for the week-ends.

Over these years I piled up an enormous amount of material, Pares even more. He went off to rifle the archives of the West Indies, and those on his subject in Boston and New York. A fast worker, he emerged with a manuscript of 300,000 words. It was not a book but an abortion. Out of it G.N. Clark and Namier excavated two books, and two substantial articles for the *English Historical Review*. It was odd that Richard had had no hunch for his subject. Kenneth Bell of Balliol and a former Fellow said the word – 'Sugar' – and Richard bought it. He became our best authority on the English eighteenth century, but, again curiously, he had no warmth for his subject. He was a singularly disillusioned man.

My subject grew upon me quite naturally. My aim was to discover what the Reformation came to in fact, what it did in detail in a small area under the microscope of minute research. Clearly my native Cornwall, with its 'difference', indicated itself, and Sir Charles Firth one evening at dinner supplied the title, 'Tudor Cornwall'. In the course of research, which seemed endless, I noticed a significant gap. There was no biography of a leading figure, Sir Richard Grenville, and eventually I discovered why. All the family and personal papers had been destroyed, which made it difficult to bring him alive – no letters to his wife or friends. So, taking a leaf out of Macaulay's note-book, I set myself to visit the places where he had lived his vigorous, assertive life, the houses, churches, monuments, portraits of the people he had known. At Bideford, his home port, everything had been destroyed too. There was no direct English account of the last fight in the Azores. It occurred to me that there must be a Spanish one. Lying about on the beach at home one summer – illish, hoping to get better – I learned enough Spanish to read Fernandez Duro's history of the Spanish Armada. This referred to the relevant documents in the Museo Geografico in Madrid, just in time before the ghastly Spanish Civil War closed everything down.

There were other technical problems about that book, which I will not go into. But just before it came out the publication was forestalled by an ordinary book-maker who made not a bad job of it. Just my luck, I thought. It killed my book in USA. Resentment at always finding things against me, always having to struggle *against*, piled up. Eventually my book established itself as the standard biography of that Elizabethan hero (he was not a nice man), and it went into several editions.

Richard was not pleased. He did not think much of biography. I took no notice – little did I care for academic fashion, or discouraging opinions. G.M. Trevelyan said to me that at Cambridge he had the impression that the medieval historians were all looking over each other's shoulders. 'They sting each other into frustration' was my phrase for it. Actually, writing a biography was good experience for a trial run, since chronological structure was already given. If I had not written *Sir Richard Grenville* first I might not have been able to accomplish a portrait of the society of Tudor Cornwall. If I had not had the experience of the latter I might not have been able to tackle a portrait of the whole society of Elizabethan England later with my trilogy.

For myself I registered, Never pay attention to others' discouragements. 'Il y a toujours quelque chose dans les malheurs de nos meilleurs amis qui ne nous déplaît pas', said La Rochefoucauld, who knew. I once said to John Sparrow, another discourager, that everything went wrong in my life – this was accumulated resentments, perhaps unfair – but that everything went right with my work.

Now that Richard was getting married and going out of College I should be lonelier than ever. I hated my friends getting married, since I was not giving any 'hostages to fortune'. I was convinced that, if fortune could get one in at me, it would. My greatest Cornish friend, Charles Henderson of Corpus, had died on his honeymoon. Now Richard ... I was the last person to know that he was even getting engaged, and, though he was my greatest friend in College, I never knew about his earlier love-affair with Evelyn Waugh. They all regarded me as an innocent. And indeed I was, wrapped up in my work and, privately, in poetry. The afternoon I learned that I was losing Richard I spent in the church of St Thomas-by-the-railway-station, in tears.

With Richard away, engulfed in married life and a conventional academic career, I saw much more of Bruce McFarlane of Magdalen, where, failing All Souls, he had become a tutorial Fellow. Following my political lead, together we brought back A.J.P. Taylor from Manchester as his colleague. In the event this turned out badly, and from Bruce I learned everything that went on in Magdalen. I also learned about the fifteenth century – Bruce had nothing to learn from me about the sixteenth century, any more than Richard had done. Why not? They showed no interest, and I had an inkling why. But Bruce took me about the countryside, and indeed the country. We would take a bus out from Oxford, and then walk, sandwiches in pocket and I always with a notebook. O those delicious walks – up the Cherwell valley to its source at Cherwellton, a lonely church by its well in the fields; from Thame, with splendid church (not for us the 'Spread Eagle' of Waugh and his friends), and across fields to Elizabethan Rycote. Out to South Leigh with its frescoed church, into the Cotswolds with the exquisite stonework of its manor-houses; or lonely Chastleton, looking over the Vale of the Red Horse beckoning to Stratford.

He took me further afield – he always had to do the organising and lead, I simply fell in with his plans. To Lincoln, to stop at Richard II's White Hart; into Bruce's native Devon to unspoiled Torbryan and Ipplepen. To Canterbury, and Ramsgate in pursuit of Pugin; on to Dover – not in pursuit of Auden and E.M. Forster's naval targets, but always in pursuit of history, historic places and monuments.

Bruce was a friend of Helena Wright, the sexologist, and got her husband to take over my near-hopeless case. This meant a couple of desperate operations in University College Hospital in London. A long stay there – so I missed all the celebrations of our Quincentenary at All Souls. Dear Warden Adams – Isaiah could do a turn of him coming into the smoking-room with news of my condition: 'He has taken a little milk.'

How kind the old boys were! When I came out of hospital Salter took me for a slow, stopping tour around Wales. We ended up at Criccieth, where we spent a day with the Lloyd Georges. 'You listen to him,' said Dame Margaret, boss in that household. 'I have had many ministers,' said the great man, 'some of them good, others indifferent. But the only one who totally and completely failed at his job – that man was Neville Chamberlain.' He had been brought in to direct recruitment for National Service, broke down on it, and handed in his cards. We were all agreed about Neville Chamberlain.

Once more the Betting Book gives us glimpses of what was being thought in College. 'March 11, 1938. Rees [Goronwy] bets Robertson 2 to 1 in half-crowns that Schuschnigg will be alive on Monday morning, March 14th.' At any rate he survived the brow-beating to which he was subjected by Hitler. 'March 18, 1938. Macartney bets Radcliffe-Brown that the UK will not go to war within 3 calendar months of the day of making this bet.' Macartney was a Trinity, Cambridge man whom Pares and I had proposed for a Research Fellowship. He had written a book on post-War Austria, and became the leading authority on Hungary – he did not think highly of A.J.P. Taylor's excursions into that area. I recruited Macartney to write the volume on Maria Theresa in my series.

'May 15, 1939. Radcliffe-Brown bets Rowse and Davies [killed, young, in the War in the Pacific] that Mr Chamberlain will still be Prime Minister three years from this date.' What an innocent the anthropologist was! No judgment, he always lost his bets, and always paid up like a gentleman. He belonged to the Trinity group of Rationalists, Russell and Trevelyan, and believed nothing – except that Shakespeare's works were written by the Earl of Oxford. To question that made him hot under the collar, and he could trot out the usual nonsense that had no doubt impressed Cape Town and Sydney. He flushed with annoyance when I questioned this rubbish – it was the only time I ever saw him angry. It was evidently a psychotic case and, ferreting as usual, I found out the psychological, non-rational, explanation. As a boy he had been brought up by an aunt at Stratford-on-Avon: this was the form that his revolt against authority took, against the tutelary deity there. All ordinary people's thinking is almost equally silly, but one did not expect that nonsense from a Cambridge Rationalist.

'February 4, 1939. Malcolm, Faber and Foster bet Jones 1/– each against 2/6 that, in the course of 1939, there will not be a war involving any two (or more) of the following countries in hostilities with one another, viz. Great Britain, France, Germany, Italy, Swinton to rule.' Geoffrey Faber paid up. The gangster of genius was, like Napoleon, a gambler.

'February 16, 1939. Harold Butler bets Rohan Butler [father and son] 2/6 that, despite all ideological inhibitions, Mr Chamberlain and his colleagues will have bound themselves in some kind of defensive alliance to the USSR before May 1, 1939.' Alas, they never would, though it was the only way to stop Hitler in his tracks. 'June 18, 1939. Hudson bets Macartney two pengoes [1/–] that Danzig will have been incorporated in the German Reich without a European war by All Souls Day 1939' [i.e. 2 November].

'July 11, 1939. Macartney bets Cox [who became a Fellow of Univ.] 4 to 1 in shillings that Britain will not have concluded a disgraceful peace with Germany by 31.12.'39. In case of dispute as to the interpretation of the words "disgraceful" or "peace" Brierly to decide.' J.L. Brierly, a Prize Fellow who had come back as Professor of International Law, was the most just of men. He recognised the territorial clauses of Versailles as essentially just. As against the rancour worked up against Versailles, it had re-created Poland and the Baltic States, and liberated the Slavs of Central and Southern Europe. The attacks on Versailles, broadcast by Keynes's damaging book, were a powerful aid to Hitler's propaganda, of which he was a master.

'September 14, 1939. Pares bets Hudson a shilling that Woodward will still be domestic bursar of this College when Hitler is no longer Führer of the German Reich.' Not so. Woodward left us, to become Professor of International Relations, and Fellow of Balliol. As domestic bursar he had put a fast one across Balliol. The College port, in the cellars under the Codrington next the boilers, had lost its bloom. Woodward sold it to Balliol, which was too high-minded to notice – 'low living and high thinking' their motto. On becoming a Fellow of Balliol the Abbé had to drink it.

'October 8, 1939. Robertson bets Harris an even half-crown that before All Souls Day 1939, Germany will have invaded Holland and Belgium.' 'April 4, 1940. Robertson bets G.N. Clark 2/6 that the Germans will make a serious offensive on the Western Front on or before May 1, 1940.' Robertson was out by only a few days. The German avalanche was upon us – really a renewal of their almighty effort in 1914-1918.

E.L. Woodward was not, strictly speaking, an Appeaser. Yet I was disappointed that, as an historian, he did not speak out against it, as his fellow historian Namier did. Woodward knew quite well what the German record was, from the time of Bismarck onwards. He had written a standard book on the German challenge to Britain's naval security leading up to 1914. He had an appointment within the Foreign Office as editor of our Diplomatic Documents between the two wars. When the second War came about – much more effectively prepared for by Hitler than by his precursors – Woodward wrote a thoroughly defeatist prognostication, which was circulated by the Foreign Office – to the dismay and indignation of the very able Hankey, Secretary to the Cabinet. He took a more balanced view of the prospects, estimating our chances. He condemned Woodward's paper as 'bad history, bad politics, bad propaganda, and grossly untrue'.[2] He deplored the circulation of a 'defeatist document at a time when defeatism is rampant'. Woodward argued that we had lost supremacy in the air – the Battle of Britain was just about to prove that that was not so; that our situation was just as if, in the struggle against Napoleon, we had lost the battle of Trafalgar. However, the Royal Navy retained its

[2] S. Roskill, *Hankey, III, 1931-1963*, 370.

supremacy. Hankey regarded Woodward's summing-up as 'all exaggerated and misleading'.

Nevertheless the Foreign Office kept him on as editor of their series of Diplomatic Documents. He recruited as assistant (and eventual successor) our junior Fellow, Rohan Butler, who had a more candid estimation of the Germans. I did not have an exaggerated opinion of Woodward as an historian, though we got on well enough when he was prepared to be youthful and giggle with Pares and me. No doubt he thought that I was uppish and needed repressing – no allowance made that I was ill, and frantic with anxiety. With me he was apt to be pompous, and suffered from the English vocational disease of superciliousness. In the Thirties he regularly pooh-poohed Hitler, as had Simon and others. At least I never made that mistake. After reading *Mein Kampf* I realised that Hitler meant what he said and had set out there what he intended to attempt.

I had a higher opinion of G.N. Clark as an historian – though disappointed by his being anti-Churchill. Where did he get that bias from? It was the more disappointing in that our relations were close and affectionate. Still, one knew his weakness, as his family did: he suffered from cold feet. I could have been described as a Churchillian Labour man: nothing odd in that, it could have done as well for Ernest Bevin – certainly nothing 'maverick', as Ben Pimlott describes it. After all, it was the Churchillians and Labour people who came together in 1940 to save the country, only just in time.

❖

To return to 1935: the 'National' government, effectively Tory in little disguise, renewed their seemingly permanent hold on power. They got a disproportionate majority, some 400 to Labour's mere 155, by a fraudulent appeal: they would adhere to Collective Security against Mussolini's aggression on Abyssinia – and then renegued on it, as Stafford Cripps said they would. Amery admitted that it was a fraud; then gently ticked me off for repeating it.

I stood again for my home constituency and got the Liberal at last to the bottom of the poll. In 1945 the seat went Labour – after all the work I had put in during the appalling Thirties: if I had not given up, I should have been 'in', and that would have been fatal. The doctors made me drop it, made me reconcile myself to a semi-invalid life. I dropped politicking, and was happy – so far as that was concerned – ever after.

I loathed the business of being a political candidate – trying to make bricks without straw, with the Labour Party, which had no sense of power. In that like the ineffective Left all over Europe. How much energy and strength I had wasted on it! I had given up most of my vacations to it, when my friends and contemporaries were having a good time on the Continent, Pares and Connolly, Evelyn Waugh, Peter Quennell, Geoffrey Hudson and Charles Henderson who died in Italy.

I was examining for the Fellowship and, in the hurry to get home for the Election, found at the railway station that I hadn't enough cash for the journey. The only person I knew on the platform was Simon, so I raised a quid off him. 'My dear fellow, what about two?' It now occurs to me that I do not remember ever repaying him. A typical story in our folk-lore related to G.D.H. Cole, who detested Simon, and made a song of it. Simon meeting him on the railway platform insisted, with bogus bonhomie, on sharing his presumed third-class (in those days) compartment. When the ticket collector came round they both showed up first-class tickets.

Meanwhile, one blow we could aim at the old men of the sea – Eden afterwards said, 'You've no idea how awful they were' – was offered by the university constituency. We might get an anti-Government candidate in. The official

Conservative candidate was our Cruttwell, but a Christ Church group put up Professor Lindeman. So the Tories were divided: here was our chance. Salter was really a Liberal, but could be put up as a non-Party candidate. I backed him for one of the two seats, and exerted myself to get the Labour candidate, Cole, to stand down for him. Geoffrey Hudson and I joined an unofficial committee to back Salter, and all pulling together we got him elected.

For the other seat, though a Labour candidate, I publicly supported the Conservative Cruttwell. He was not only an All Souls man but a Churchillian, not a Chamberlainite, and a good head on military affairs should be useful in Parliament in the growing urgency. In the event both Lindeman and Cruttwell – each of whom would have been useful – were defeated. This unexpected blow had a bad psychological effect on Cruttwell; he felt that the Oxford Tories had deliberately let him down, and he nursed the wound. Here one should put right the misrepresentation of him by his pupil, Evelyn Waugh. Waugh never allowed for the fact that Cruttwell had been invalided by the War. Before 1914 he had been a hearty, rugger-playing athlete. Now, after the Western Front, he was riddled with arthritis, lamed and I don't know what besides. In the History School he was a leading figure; as an examiner he had awarded me my First and Evelyn his Third. Evelyn caricatured Cruttwell by name in several of his books. Evelyn was a drunk and a waster; all Cruttwell said to me peaceably was: 'I could have sent him down.' He never did. Cruttwell was a Christian and a gentleman, neither of which terms could be accorded to Evelyn.

I now made over my claim to the best double set of rooms in the inner quad to Salter, who made fullest use of them. I clung to my old dark rooms in the old quad, in spite of the grim memory in my bedroom which had terrified me for years – I was determined not to give in, even if I could not exorcise it. Salter, now an MP, entertained. One week-end he had Churchill down. I was away, but I learned how Winston had inveighed against Baldwin as 'a whited sepulchre'. Baldwin may have read my attack on him in the *Political Quarterly*, for he excused himself to his friend Pember on the ground that he was holding down a job for which he was physically incapable. Well, he should have brought in Churchill – the only thing that either Hitler or Stalin would take notice of. When G.M. Young was called in to write Baldwin's biography and stayed with him at Bewdley, he admitted that he detested him – I never understood quite why. Perhaps it was the humbug, of which Baldwin was a past-master, as well as masterly party-manoeuvrer, but one could hardly dislike the private man. Young may have been further to the Left than I realised.[3] Salter once got Horace Wilson down, Chamberlain's *éminence grise*, Head of the Civil Service. No response in that quarter, determinedly heading for the rocks.

Naturally, from Salter's war-time experience of acute shortages of materials, he thought we should be building up essential stocks. So he got together a committee on which economists like Walter Layton figured, along with unattached birds like Harold Nicolson and Lord Allen of Hurtwood. I attended. But to what point? Nothing offered much hope of action while the old men of the sea held on. They really regarded themselves as indispensable, and privately called Churchill's group 'the gangsters'! Dawson called the blameless Salter, no politician, a 'rabble-rouser'.

The war came down upon us in the worst of all circumstances. Under the able Liberal Government of 1914 we confronted the enemy in alliance with France, Russia, Italy and soon half Europe. After twenty years of Tory ascendancy we were alone, with a France we had helped to

[3] For example, he thought better of Laski's political theorising, and of Spender's Leftist poeticising, than I did.

demoralise with the ill-considered Anglo-German Naval Pact, handing Hitler an early victory, the first of many. The fall of France came as a thunderclap: now Britain was in acute danger. No one expected that. Lionel Curtis: 'We must go down with our flags flying.' Four French high naval officers were entertained in College, after the surrender, being repatriated. They were all anti-British, so far as I could sense, and certainly expected the fall of Britain.

At this juncture Salter unexpectedly got married to the formidable American lady who had been gunning for him for years at Geneva. Now, running him down in England, at this juncture, in the midst of clamour and crisis, she got him. At this his scout in College gave voice: 'What next? First the fall of France – and now *this!*'

Salter was nature's bachelor, though he would have liked to marry Ka Arnold-Forster. Rupert Brooke had been her lover, and John Sparrow was supposed to be editing the love-letters. He never did. Salter shared house in the bachelor establishment of two aesthetes, Archie Balfour and Robertson of the Ashmolean. Driving me out to lunch, Archie Balfour tried to argue me into agreeing that Appeasement was the right policy. I was affronted by this from a third-rate brain; by the time we arrived we were hardly on speaking terms. His brother, Jock Balfour in the Foreign Office, knew better.

Much as I disliked my friends marrying I gave Salter my moral support and a helping hand, for he needed it. The descendant of New England Cotton Mather, Ethel was a formidability in her own right, made on an ample scale, while her Arthur was small and squat. Bruce McFarlane named the toad that lived in a hole outside his gamekeeper's cottage at Wheatley 'Sir Arthur Salter'. Ethel thought the name pretty, and pretended to deplore his elevation to the peerage. I said he could put a P to his name and become Lord Psalter.

With Arthur out of College I at last succeeded to those

grand rooms, an innermost sanctum. I was less happy at succeeding to Tonge, when I had been faithfully looked after by my honest Aubrey Lewendon for twenty years. Not the brightest of men, he had arrived one morning with my tea and the exciting news 'S 'as landed'. What? Who? Where? I was already awake and reading my letters, but couldn't make it out. 'S', affirmed Aubrey, 'Party-leader S'. At last it dawned on me that this was no less than Hitler's deputy, Hess, who had landed.

My old rooms had the equivocal memory of Adam von Trott. We did not know what to think of him now; he was working in the Nazi Foreign Office, for the destabilisation of British rule in India. He once mentioned to me that Germany was restricted in Europe and needed living space. What was this but Hitler's *Lebensraum*; and what about the people, Poles, Slavs, inhabiting it? He had the German faculty of creating trouble around him, and I had dropped him. He had not lost his singular faculty of making up to people – the Astors, Lothian, Halifax. He later redeemed himself as a key-figure in the aristocrats' Resistance, along with more impressive Helmut von Moltke, to whom I had introduced him one sombre autumn evening at dinner in Hall. Lionel Curtis took up Helmut, as I had taken up Adam. But – Resistance? There was not the slightest support from the German people at large for the aristocrats' attempt – too late – on Hitler's life.

Adam made up to Warden Adams: sadly, from my window I saw the tall figure loping into the Lodgings. No response in that quarter. Anyway Adams was not interested in foreign affairs; he was far too busy with good works at home. Impossible to enumerate the bodies on which he served: Chairman of Social Services for Great Britain and the Young Farmers took up most of his time. He once said to me that he had been 'broken in', good country image. I knew what that meant: my father had been good at 'breaking in' horses and ponies, though not me.

1. Lord Curzon

2. Lord Halifax

3. W.P. Ker

4. Sir Charles Oman

5. Leopold Amery

6. Hensley Henson

7. Lord Simon

8. Archbishop Lang

9. T.E. Lawrence by
Augustus John

10. G.N. Clark

11. Reggie Harris

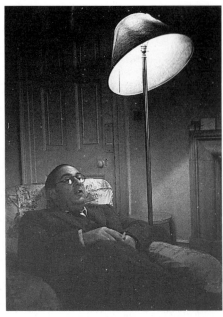

12. Richard Pares

13. Isaiah Berlin

14. Warden Anson

15. Warden Sumner

16. Warden Sparrow

17. Looking into the Common-Room garden

18. The Codrington Library

19. Showing Konrad Adenauer around the college

20. Receiving Vincent Auriol at Encaenia

21. Encaenia luncheon
in the Codrington

22. The author in his rooms

4. Warden Adams

Warden Adams would not accept any recognition of his lifelong public work. He turned down knighthoods; in the end Mrs Adams had to make him accept a C.H. He was the most selfless of men, his background the good Scotch dominie of a parent to whom David Livingstone entrusted his son when he was in Africa. When asked what he meant to become, the boy answered 'a missionary in Africa' like his father. I think that he gave his life fighting against slavery in the American Civil War. Warden Adams was as good a raconteur as Warden Pember, except that he had little time for it. Nor for the arts, though it was a pointer that he particularly liked Rembrandt, of all painters the most dedicated to humanity; and, in contemporary literature, *John Brown's Body*.

Muriel Adams did her duty no less nobly. She said to me that, in a marriage, one had to go under, and she had gone under. She did her best to entertain, in all the difficulties of the war. There was a dinner-party for Lang, who had come down to take the chair at some ecumenical conference. After dinner the Archbishop came back, needlessly, but now arrayed in doctoral scarlet as well as episcopal purple to make the round of the ladies like a prince of the Church. So far from genuflecting, the Warden's sister, a spry Scotch spinster, said as the purple and scarlet withdrew: 'To think that my mother called *his* mother Hannah!'

Lang's father had been Moderator of the Presbyterian Kirk of Scotland. This meant that the son was looked upon askance up there when he became an Anglican, High Church too. When he reached York, all his Scotch ghilly said was: 'Weel, ye've a gran' fine kirk noo.' Archbishop Davidson had been Presbyterian too, but Low Church, a simple Evangelical believer, no such inner conflict as Lang had with himself. Pember was once at an evening party with his friend Davidson when a devout young lady came up to genuflect and kiss his ring, as if he were a Roman. The poor Archbishop had to put up with it, but apologised to Pember with a grimace.

Pember was no less anti-Puseyite. He once told me that Pusey had blurted out information he had heard in confession. Very improper. I used to tease chaplain Brooke, sensibly Low Church, that he would have to hear my confession if I demanded it. He admitted that he would have to, but hoped that he would not be called upon. I had always been interested in the Oxford Movement, and made a collection of Newman's first editions. When David Cecil married I gave him my first edition of the *Apologia pro vita sua*, not too unsuitably for, like all the Cecils, he was High Church and even *croyant*.

My new rooms were not only more comfortable but offered new inspiration. Why had I not translated myself before? – not strong enough to face moving all my books and possessions. Now I had light and cream-painted panelling, Georgian rooms designed by Hawksmoor. On one side I looked out across the wide lawn to the dome of the Radcliffe Camera and Aldrich's spire of All Saints. On the other I looked down into the Warden of New College's garden: a Naboth's vineyard, for it had formerly belonged to All Souls, which had exchanged it for a piece the Codrington had been built upon. I wished that we could get it back, for we had only a tiny patch of the garden left to us, for sitting out of doors. I now had the long range of Queen's Library in full view, a superb copper beech, and the inspiration of the East. There were the two sides of my life – poetry and research – expressed in the poem written at the time, 'The Choice'. In the war now upon us I was not in a 'reserved occupation'. I was at once rejected at my medical examination and dismissed. I felt an odd pang, the feeling of forever being outside, outside of life, everything. Then I volunteered to Ernest Bevin's Ministry of Labour; he recommended me to try Harold Nicolson's Ministry of Information, no friend of mine. It was all for the good; I was not up to scratch physically; even our amateur fire-drill, with a reservoir in the middle of the quad, brought on a slight haemorrhage. The only thing to get on with was writing: no pupils now, in a deserted Oxford, I could concentrate on that.

How propitious those rooms were for work-work-work. I was next door to the Codrington, could descend there at any time of day or night for the books I wanted, could find my way to the proper shelves practically in the dark – though then an echo in the roof made my too-exposed nerves shudder. The Bodleian was just across the road. In London I had worked only at manuscripts, for years, at the PRO and the Manuscript Room of the British Museum, not the famous Reading Room of Panizzi, Marx and Lenin, of Richard Garnett and my favourite Samuel Butler.

Freed in spirit, the work went forward, my historical writing! Not *A Cornish Childhood*, which I wrote at home in the charming house on the Bay, which someone conveniently evacuated for fear of invasion in 1940. 'Polmear Mine' was a source of new inspiration too; my cloud was lifting. In spite of the danger to the country, the bombs that fell on the little ports near us, the 1940s were not as hapless and hopeless as the 1930s. The best people from both sides – Churchillian Tories and my Labour people, Ernest Bevin and Clem Attlee – had come together to save the country at the last gasp. I had not been so far wrong after all – as people had thought. Politically, I was happy: I could give up, and give myself to work, and the inspiration of those inspired days.

Churchill had never forgiven the Chamberlainites. So far as he could, he kicked them upstairs. Simon he relegated to the Woolsack he had rejected twenty years before, but he never took him into the War Cabinet. Halifax he ousted from the Foreign Office, and sent him off to Washington to succeed the popular Lothian. When Lothian died of his Christian Science there, a convert of Nancy Astor's from Catholicism (how erratic he was!), his friend Curtis pronounced his epitaph: 'Philip died in the knowledge that he had been wrong.'

The College was well represented in the decisive war-effort at Washington. Salter did a great job again in directing the immense programme of ship-building to combat the renewed, and vastly increased, German submarine menace. Brand was there to cope with our financial needs. Harold Butler and John Foster in Information services. So was the bright young Berlin whose live reports on American opinion recommended him to Churchill. Wishing to meet the author, he invited Berlin to lunch at 10 Downing Street. Both were nonplussed to find that the Berlin who turned up was Irving Berlin, the composer, but of music.

With the end of the war Adams's Wardenship came to an end. He retired to Ireland, where by the lough the tinkle of the chapel bell had precisely the tone of the Chapel bell at All Souls, which he had attended faithfully, to remind him.

CHAPTER 5

Warden Sumner

In 1945 we elected Benedict Humphry Sumner Warden. Though a Balliol man, he was very much a Wykehamist. All Souls, electing its Prize Fellows from other colleges, constituted a kind of barometer as to their standing and, after the nineteenth-century reforms, how good they were academically. Before these, in old unreformed Oxford, All Souls was largely recruited from aristocratic Christ Church. Roger Makins and I were both House men elected together. Never again. The Christ Church contribution was down to a trickle, with a poor record in the Schools.

Jowett's Balliol was acutely competitive and became the top college academically. So, up to 1914, All Souls was dominantly Balliol, with a strong contingent of Etonians. Between the two wars New College, a Wykehamist foundation, went ahead. At one time just after the second War I counted an actual majority of Wykehamists in College, whether from New College (like Jacob, Sparrow, Wilberforce, Jay), or from Balliol (like Sumner and Pares). We were now equipped with a Wykehamist Warden and College officers, Domestic Bursar, and Librarian.

Sumner had served in the first War and then had a brief spell at Geneva, but was an academic of the purest water. He had served some twenty years as a tutorial Fellow of Balliol, then was briefly a professor at Edinburgh, from which he was summoned to become Warden – at which he was a bit overwhelmed. His sights were largely fixed on the university – a contrast with Adams, Chelmsford, Pember.

Tall, handsome, and dark with a Disraelian cast of countenance and a long loping stride, he was a deeply reticent, inhibited man. He had a remarkable background, with an archbishop and a bishop in it, and a distinguished father never mentioned whom nobody knew about. Heywood Sumner was a Pre-Raphaelite artist, a mosaicist, whose work can be seen in the churches of Sussex. He became a notable archaeologist of the New Forest. The family background was odd, self-consciously aesthetic, somewhat Puritan, inhibited. David Cecil described it to me, and would say: 'Why can't Humphry say, "Damn it, I've dropped my cigarette"?' Unthinkable – impossible for him to let himself go so far.

Nature's bachelor, he had to have his sister to keep house for him. He couldn't bear it, but needs must. Her appearance was striking, and distinctly masculine: she wore the trousers. From a College party, the demotic wife of one of the new post-War generation inquired: 'Who was that old woman who looked like a bloody wizard?' O tempora, O mores! The times, and indeed the College, were changing. No more grand entertaining in the Lodgings. The Sumners were not well off. But indeed the times were bad. The country was exhausted by its long struggle – in which its historic greatness, as I wrote at the time, went out in heroic flames. War-time rations continued; fuel was scarce; we were cold. It was a bleak time, and I found Humphry, though noble and suffering, a bleak man. 'Manners makyth man', indeed: it unmade him as a man. His courtesy was impeccable, but everything was deliberate, considered, controlled, to an inhuman extent. It must have been bad for him. He was the most unhappy man I have ever known.

I hadn't the word for it then, but in fact he was a masochist. I thought of him innocently as just 'inside-out'. If anything was in *his* interest he took the opposite line, and went against it. We were to transform the manciple's house, opposite the Warden's Lodgings: Humphry favoured an outsize building which would have overlooked his garden and spoiled his view. Like that about everything. I observed it when he came down to stay with me in Cornwall. It made me impatient. I then found that he was a fellow duodenal, and had the symptoms. He was a worrier; he worried us all, and himself to death, poor fellow, for of course he was a good man and a nice one, though cool, not warm-hearted like dear Adams. He was no less self-less, indeed he might be described as being anti-self.

This came up over the estates bursarship. Over many years Faber had made a good thing of it, and we were flush. He bought for us an estate at Minsted in Hampshire, where he built up a pedigree herd, and resided. Was it the College's business to go in for direct farming? John Foster thought not, and whenever it came up, put the argument against it. For it cost subsidy after subsidy, while Faber built up his farm and herd. He had the backing of Warden Adams, whose heart was in farming and couldn't resist cattle.

Geoffrey Faber made a name for himself as one of the most promising new publishers. He had survived the war, before which he had served a publishing apprenticeship with the University Press. A red-faced Rugbeian with shining proboscis, he had a quick temper, also a fund of obstinacy which served him well in the uphill struggle to found a firm with little capital. He had the estates bursarship as a raft to hold on to, and he held on to it for more than twenty years, until his firm made its name – and his.

At first the going was rough. One of the former Fellows put some capital into the little firm, which began as Faber and Gwyer, who then withdrew it. What should the firm's new name be? Geoffrey tried it out on me, at dinner in Hall

– 'Faber and Faber'. I registered at once that it did the trick.

All Souls provided another resource to him as a recruiting ground for authors. There was W.K. Hancock waiting in the wings. Faber published his first book, about Ricasoli and the Risorgimento in Tuscany. Hancock never completed the work, but went on to other subjects. He managed with dexterity a double career between England and Australia, holding professorships in both, while at times returning to All Souls. During the second War he worked in government offices by day, and fire-watched at St Paul's by night. He wrote the official biography of Smuts, who visited us – a commanding figure, steely profile and eyes – as also did Herzog, a less impressive person, and charming Jan Hofmeyr, who was meant for Smuts's successor but died young.

Faber also published a couple of Indian stories by our humourless old Anglo-Indian guest, Sir Henry Sharp. Then there came my juvenile *Politics and the Younger Generation*, over which Eliot took so much trouble, in his conscientious way. He took more trouble over the manuscript than it deserved, but on one point I disagreed. The impulse for the book came partly from my consciousness of the loss to the country of the generation before mine – there they were, as I have said, on the walls, Raymond Asquith, Shaw-Stewart and the rest, who should have been alive to lead the country in the 'locust years'. Eliot was unaware of this, and inserted that only two men of genius were lost – the sculptor Gaudier-Brzeska and T.E. Hulme, a cult figure of theirs. It showed how restricted Eliot's view was at the time, largely confined to fellow-American Pound's group.

Years later, in the second German war, André Gide met De Gaulle in Algiers. De Gaulle was regretting that he had not enough men under his command. Gide made the grim comment that they were all under their wooden crosses in the war cemeteries of France. This was the historic fact: the Germans bled France white in their first War. Britain's loss was also grievous.

My book was caught in the panic Election of 1931, and that put paid to that. Both Eliot's and my efforts were a total loss. Still, it meant co-operation, and much I owed to him. Faber published Eliot's *Criterion*, and he kept me regularly at it, reviewing and writing articles on my obsession with political, especially Marxist, theory. My next move was a disappointment to Faber. He expected to publish my *Sir Richard Grenville of the 'Revenge'*. But that needed the oversight of the leading Elizabethan historian of the day, Professor J.E. Neale, who took the book to Cape, for whom he was reader. However, Eliot took my poetry under his wing, and himself wrote the blurbs for the first three volumes. He was a regular writer of blurbs, and built up a commanding position for Faber as a publisher of verse. I suggested Roy Campbell to him, putting forward his *Adamastor*. When Eliot died, his standards were not maintained by his successors, whose choices became erratic, as Larkin observed

Faber continued to publish books for our junior fellows. He published Rohan Butler's remarkable *The Roots of National Socialism*. Very mature for so young a man, Butler at least knew, as an historian, what to expect from the Germans. It was natural too that Geoffrey should publish Goronwy Rees's first two ventures into fiction: Geoffrey was devoted to him, and others too found Goronwy's Celtic charm irresistible. His second book, *A Bridge to Divide Them*, was patently autobiographical: one recognised the talk of his little group, Douglas Jay, Peggy Garnett and Sheila Grant-Duff. Though I became Jay's life-long friend, I was not one of their group – and observed Goronwy with a critical eye. Why didn't he stick to his last? Why didn't he carry on with his fictional beginning? To be just, he may not have had the gift. But he never had the character to stick to one line: his broken, equivocal career was a succession of different stops and starts. When young, and with his looks, he had all the luck; half-way through, luck turned against him and he had more than his share of misfortune.

I can see a typical encounter now. Summer Sunday morning: Headlam in apron and gaiters, top-hat with episcopal strings attached, on his way to choral matins at Christ Church. Young Goronwy, open-neck blue shirt to go with violet blue eyes, wavy black hair rather dishevelled from tennis, equipped with racket, all the bells of Oxford ringing to Sunday service. Headlam, at this apparition at the gate: 'You are very *beautiful* this morning, Rees!' Was a reproach intended? Goronwy goes by with a sulky toss of the head.

Since Faber was estates bursar we saw more of him than of most of the London element. He was oddly accident-prone, and that added to the gaiety of his visits. On one of his tours of College estates he took the risk of charging his car – he was an impulsive man – into an overswollen ford. The car stalled; Geoffrey had to get out, and wade across to get help, the water almost up to his waist. On another occasion he was fishing in a high wind. The wind blew the barb of his fishing-line back into his face; the hook caught in the gristle of his nose, the more he tried to extract it the more it swelled up. Eventually he mounted his motor-bicycle to go and find a doctor in the neighbouring town. He made a comic spectacle riding with fishing-rod-and-line attached to his face, the boys in the street hooting at him as he progressed up the hill to a surgery.

Few fishermen were left in College to take advantage of the stretch of fishing we owned on the pretty stream, the Windrush, which runs down the valley from Burford. Reggie Harris made a few attempts upon it, otherwise it was neglected and deteriorated. A more professional fisherman was Ernest Jacob, who fished the Ribble in

Lancashire regularly. Thence he dispatched a large salmon from time to time for our kitchen. In my innocence I used to think it a gift – but though he was then domestic bursar and would be eating it gratis, he charged for it.

Lionel Curtis was another who was accident-prone. So too the absent-minded Geoffrey Hudson. Hudson was said to have travelled up to London in his carpet slippers. Several times coming back from Paddington by the midnight train he overshot Oxford station. He would wake up and find himself at Banbury, where he waited for hours on the bleak platform for the early morning milk-train into Oxford. Curtis was travelling back, during the first German war, through the Mediterranean when there was a submarine alert. He went below to console an old lady who was rather hysterical, and sat down on her crochet-bag on the chair beside her. The crochet-needle penetrated his behind and could not be got out. So Lionel had to make his way up the companion-way to the ship's surgeon, crochet-bag and all attached to his bottom. People laughed so much that they forgot about the submarine.

One way and another Faber's may be thought of as an interesting extension of All Souls into the literary world. Geoffrey one day said to me that, if he were to be remembered, it would be for having saved Tom Eliot for literature.

Now Faber, a satisfied power, was giving up, and wanted to hand over to Rees. But was Goronwy the right man for the job? Neither Sparrow, who was his friend, nor I thought so. I had taken his measure long ago. When he came into College, handsome and seductive, a playboy, everybody fell for him. I was sympathetic as a fellow-Leftist, though mistaken in thinking him a fellow-proletarian; we were both Celts, for he was Welsh, but middle-class. Faber noted how very different we were, but all his affection was for Goronwy. Women fell for him too – notably Elizabeth Bowen – and he for them.

He needed a subject to qualify for a Research Fellowship. I thought up a suitable one for him: the Leftist Lassalle, rival of Marx, opponent of Bismarck, brilliant and gifted, an adventurer and womaniser. This gave Goronwy the excuse to go to Germany, where he had a good time with the boys, did nothing, came back and handed in his cards. Thereupon John Sparrow and I got him a job as assistant literary editor of the *Spectator*. He could now have a good time in London. He was a light-weight, an irresponsible. Though devoutly hetero, he was a close friend of Guy Burgess, whom once, as we have seen, he brought into the smoking-room to drink after dinner. I never spoke to Burgess. He and his lot wouldn't have approved of a sober Labour man, a follower of Ernest Bevin. I couldn't fancy Goronwy, impecunious yet extravagant, looking after the College finances. After some Left-wing meeting in London he had 'felt like oysters', so they adjourned from their Socialist gathering to Prunier's. Nor could I see Goronwy dealing with the Yorkshire farmers at Slaidburn whom Faber had found so recalcitrant about raising their rents. I had a better candidate in James Fawcett who, besides being a lawyer, had the qualification of owning a farm himself in the North Country.

Over this simple appointment Sumner held committee after committee, eventually combining two committees. I couldn't make out what or whom he wanted; and was thunder-struck when finally, after all that committee-ing, I found that he was in favour of Rees. Can he really have been? I could have stopped Rees's appointment, so many were against it, but refrained from opposing the Warden's wishes, when they ultimately emerged. Humphry was a great one for putting everything right with everyone. Afterwards he came up to my room to put it right with me; after all, he said, Rees would have him to supervise him. 'Well, it's your own funeral,' I said; and so it turned out.

5. Warden Sumner

To be fair, it appears that Goronwy was quite good at office work, and he was clever enough at presenting the estates business at College meetings. Also he had a good war record in the Welsh Fusiliers. Fawcett had an equally good record in the Navy, in the operations that rounded up the *Bismarck*. He served in the destroyer *Maori*, and felt how sad it was to see the great ship going down. (Of course in building it Hitler had broken the Anglo-German Naval Agreement.) Fawcett came back to a distinguished career at the Bar – not to College – and earned his knighthood. He would have been the right man.

*

Sumner's academic subject was Russian history, and he had written two thorough-going books in his field. With all his teaching, he over-worked, as I did. He was widely respected in the university, and quite influential. He had promoted his Balliol colleague Galbraith to be Regius Professor of Modern History; a medievalist, he was not the right man for that job. Humphry made E.F. Jacob, another medievalist, Chichele Professor of Modern History. So they had two medievalists, and no modernist. To show the flag, I allowed my name to go forward. When my old tutor, Jacob, was appointed, Humphry came up to put things right again. Would I like to be the next professor of Political Theory? No, I would not. I had lost all belief in political theorising. People's political theories were but the extrapolations of their interests. If they were supporters of monarchy, like Filmer, they put forward Divine Right. If they were opponents, like Locke, they believed in a social contract and the rights of the people. Too obvious – sickening; and I was sick of it all. I wanted only to write.

Salter's chair had been divided, and Adams had recruited G.D.H. Cole for the Political Theory professorship. Cole opted for Berlin for successor as having 'more fire in his belly'. Wisely he had dropped the will-o'-the-wisp pursuit of metaphysics for the more rewarding history of ideas. He could have written three or four substantial books for us on Russian thinkers and social thought. He never did, he devoted himself to essays, skimming the European cream; his little book on Marx was only half a book, dealing mainly with his philosophy, the least important part of him.

Isaiah was followed by Plamenatz, who really did – *mirabile dictu* – find something to say. Isaiah, protégé at Corpus of my Cornish friend Charles Henderson, was a Prize Fellow; John Plamenatz not, but he made a first-class professor of his disillusioning subject. He was a disillusioned man himself, and he wrote first-rate books. For the practical half of the subject, Political Institutions, we recruited Kenneth Wheare, and could not have done better. An expert on committees as such, on the Statute of Westminster, well seen in Whitehall, he was a master of his subject. He wrote the volume on Abraham Lincoln in my series, turning in something original. Not a chronological narrative as an historian would have done, but an analytical treatment of the different aspects of Lincoln's life and work: Illinois lawyer, the Presidency, Slavery, the Union, the Civil War.

Ken was Australian Cornish, the name Wheare means 'merry', and he was the most amusing speaker in Oxford. His Australian precursor was Keith Hancock, but the two were not friendly. Hancock was closed-up, conventional, on his guard. He had an invalid wife, whom we were not allowed to meet. He was nothing but kind to me in my first years, and on his return to Australia used me to keep him in touch with things here, arrange publication for writings of his, like his lively account of Pitcairn and the *Bounty* mutineers.

He came to and fro. Robertson appointed him to the chair of Economic History at Birmingham. After the war he contributed a hefty volume to the official history of the war effort on the economic side. But we drifted apart. A purist academic, I doubt if he liked the way I went, my Party campaigning, the personal element in my writing, or the popular success of *A Cornish Childhood*. An ambitious writer himself, with a conscious care for style, he did not know that the personal element is what makes a book *live*. His own books, all good, had no success beyond their limited appeal. Yet, when Bill de L'Isle went out as Governor General to Australia I gave him Hancock's book as the best introduction to it. To his first wife I gave the Penguin Book of Australian Verse, for I much admired Judith Wright's poetry there.

When Hancock wrote his own autobiography it was reviewed unfavourably in the *Times Literary Supplement*, not by me, but by Wheare. I understood why. For Hancock was not letting himself go, he was too self-conscious, defensive, pussy-footing. What is the point of writing an autobiography at all like that, virtuously concealing the subject?

I valued our Australian contacts, and wished that someone would write up the Australian Cornish. When Menzies visited us he told me that he was a Cornish Sampson on his mother's side. Their Attorney General, Sir Garfield Borthwick, with that improbable name, insisted that he was three-quarters Cornish. Of our Australian Fellows Dick Latham was lost in the RAF over the North Sea. Long-legged, lanky, he was a man of principle, as opposed to appeasing Hitler as he was to C.S. Lewis's theological nonsense, which had such popular appeal during the war, *The Problem of Pain* and all that. (Naturally it was an insoluble problem on his assumptions.)

Dunbabin, our noble Tasmanian, Greek historian and archaeologist, had an extraordinary war. For two or three years 'Kyrios Tom' lived up in the mountains of Crete, directing operations against the German occupation, himself never once betrayed. In the end he and his colleagues had the Germans on the run. Tom came back to us, but the long strain was beyond human endurance; it was not long before he died, still quite young.

Davies, younger still, was little more than a gay enchanting youth when he went down in the Pacific. His forbears had been missionaries in Hawaii, and the family had considerable property there. We hardly had time to know him. But we all knew dear Dick Holdsworth, the Professor's only son, tall, athletic, engaging. When he was killed in the RAF, if broke old Sir William. No consolation that he was awarded (prompted by Simon) an OM for his many-volumed *History of English Law*: it was still uncompleted, for he shortly died.

Among Jewish refugees we cared for, from the criminal barbarism in Germany, was Wolf, a recognised international lawyer. We gave him a little room along the passage into the back quad, Kitchen Court, where he worked peacefully among his books. His only son was killed in the RAF over Germany – I hope getting some of his own back. Actually, half of the Old Quad had been occupied by the US Air Force, planning the bombing of Germany. Poor Germans! They had collected the world against them, as before.

Among European grandees – sooner or later everybody seemed to turn up at All Souls – ex-Chancellor Brüning visited us. He had escaped only just in time from Hitler and Göring's murders of June 30, 1934. I have a reason for remembering it, for I asked him about the financial support Hitler had got from the Ruhr industrialists and armaments magnates. He knew nothing about it. I registered that someone in his position ought to have known; no wonder he got himself defeated by Hitler.

Similarly when Beneš turned up, I made the obvious point that Czecho-Slovakia might have absorbed, or contained, a million or so Südeten Germans, but not three millions. He agreed that it had been a mistake, but did not plead that the French had insisted on it at Versailles, as was the case.

❋

One recruit for whom Sumner was personally responsible was Jean Seznec, whom he attracted from Harvard to be professor of French Literature. The Breton Seznec, a fellow Celt, was in fact a connoisseur of the arts. He had written a classic on the Survival of the Myths of the Ancient Gods into the Renaissance, and he devoted years of scholarship to editing the works and correspondence of Diderot on the arts. I made friends with him, but he was a cold fish for a Frenchman: the name Seznec means Saxon in Breton, i.e. English.

I gradually grew to dislike examining for the Fellowship, though regularly called upon – it became so difficult to compare and assess candidates from different fields. The traditional subjects had been classics, with philosophy, to cater for Greats people; history, ancient, medieval and modern; law. Great importance was attached to an essay and a general paper, to test general intelligence. Law candidates were judged more easily, on a slightly lower level, as having less to show up in the general papers. Of course the eminent lawyers of former days had all been good classics, Simon outstanding.

To this we now added papers for Modern Greats candidates, i.e. modern philosophy, politics, and economics. Finally we added English Literature, or we should not have recruited Con O'Neill, Andrew Harvey, Peter Conrad. How to judge them all? – I found it more and more teasing. When first examining I was rather proud of capturing H.V. Hodson. It did not turn out to my advantage when he became editor of the *Sunday Times*.

There were difficulties of comparison within the same

field. Lionel Butler at Magdalen had intended to be a modernist historian, but could not put up with A.J.P. Taylor as tutor, so he became a medievalist. He wrote exuberant, fluent papers, for he had a literary flair. For his victory over Michael Howard see above p. 21.

Humphry had no favourites, but he had a *bête noire*, and that was Sparrow. Those two Wykehamists had nothing to say to each other, except that John would put baited questions to tease Humphry in College meetings. That kind of thing amused John; it did not amuse Humphry, nor did it me, who had no time for it. Nor could Humphry's reserve approve of John's openness. When John came out with a frank article about Oscar Wilde, Humphry took the opportunity to point a disapproving finger at it: 'I would not have written that.' He dared say no more, too embarrassed.

Then Sparrow came out openly in the *Lady Chatterley's Lover* case, pointing out naughtily the extra thrill the gamekeeper (Lawrence) gave to her ladyship. This amenity others had not noticed. At the same time he had not observed that, underneath D.H. Lawrence's hetero-sexual pretensions, he was basically homosexual. This was curiously imperceptive of John, and he would not take it from me when I told him. The evidence is all through Lawrence's life and work – no need to go into it here. Dorothy Brett told me that the hold which the dreadful Frieda had was simply that she made him feel more of a man than he really was. To me it was incomprehensible that John couldn't see through it all: besides being perverse, he had a contradictious streak. However, he did one day express surprise at my understanding of human beings. Not very flattering, for it meant that, from my reclusive way of life, one could not be expected to know. However, holding aloof is a good way of observing them. Swift and Henry James, my mentors, observed human beings well enough from the side.

Once only, Humphry surprised me by slipping out that

he approved my conduct of life. This meant something different. The war shattered, with much else, the repression which had driven me nearly to extinction, and was driving him. The juniors of this war-generation had no repression about the facts of life. Lionel Butler – who had served in the RAF, and was pursued to All Souls by a brave naval commander (in vain) – observed that at dessert Humphry would not touch bananas, and could not even bear to see them skinned. This young man had an observant humour. When my *Tudor Cornwall* came out he suggested that it might have for sequel Stuart Hampshire. I quoted this in a Preface, whereupon a bright young editor in a New York publishing house informed me that this was the name of a professor. I had to inform him that it was a joke.

Stuart was a New College man, though not a Wykehamist. He became involved – as so many did in wartime (Quintin Hogg too) – in a marital tangle: I will not go into it, except in so far as it came before the College, from which it kept him sadly away. Warden Sumner was paralysed with embarrassment and could give no lead. Sparrow, whom nothing daunted, took up the case, seconded by Wilberforce. I weighed in with an emotional appeal. Argument was never any good with a lot of clever Fellows who could come up with a dozen arguments in reply. Personal and private matters were no concern of other people; a young man of promise to be allowed to go to wreck. This appeal was effective with the seniors. Stuart came back, and made the best domestic bursar we ever had. He went on to succeed Maurice Bowra as Warden of Wadham. At one time there were six or seven All Souls men who were Heads of Houses in Oxford, and Warden Sparrow held a dinner for them in the Lodgings.

Besides editing my Teach Yourself History series and writing my own books, I was advising Odhams, who were hopefully entering the field of book publishing, about possible titles. This was remunerative, but frustrating. I found them a best-seller by suggesting to Alan Bullock that he write the life of Hitler. He acknowledged this in his Preface, then omitted it from subsequent editions. Why? Was it merely because I had moved away from the Left? Bullock's best-seller made the foundation for a successful career academically and on the Left.

I found them other books. Powicke's medieval essays were admirable, but scattered, not easy to find. I arranged them together in a book, which sold several thousand. Odhams could hardly credit it. Enquiring of the Oxford University Press as to his receipts from them, Powicke found that he had a balance of £25. Odhams made him several hundred pounds. The Professor then thought he could arrange a second volume of essays – and arranged it all pedantically back to front. Sir Reginald Coupland's life of Wilberforce had been left out of print; we brought it back into proper circulation in some thousands. What with all this, and my own writing, there was no time for professoring. Nor indeed any inclination for it. No pupils, no more politics, writing was all in all: my real vocation.

❖

Keith Feiling came back to All Souls at last as a professor. He had waited over-long to step into Oman's shoes. 'While there is death there is hope,' he would say. In spite of my breach with my old College, for which we both had some responsibility, I gave him a warm welcome. The second volume of his History of the Tory Party came to me for a review which pleased him. It was too favourable: he had followed the chops and changes of Whig ministries at Westminster in minute detail. This was a mistake, for the real strength of eighteenth-century Toryism was in the country, in the counties and in county towns like Exeter, York, Worcester, in cathedral cities like Dr Johnson's

Lichfield. He should have pursued the Party there.

Feiling had real feeling for history, but he was not a good writer. Compare him with Trevelyan, all of whose books had backbone, structure. Feiling's had not. On the other hand, he had a sensitive gift for thumb-nail sketches of people, which Trevelyan had not. Nor was it to be expected of G.N. Clark, who came into the smoking-room one day, chortling, 'I have at length written a book which not only no one will read, but no one can read, even if they try.' What was the point of that? Books are for reading. His volume of commercial statistics during a few years around 1690 would have done better as articles.

He was quick on the mark and quick on the move. A.J.P. Taylor tells us that he was bored with tutorial work at Oriel, and for years Alan had no good word for his tutor and used to attack him venomously. But G.N., like Arthur Bryant, had the art of feeding the hand that bit him. He was glad to get into the chair of Economic History and come back to us. Then shortly he left us to become Regius Professor of History at Cambridge. He stayed there only three years, to come back as Provost of Oriel. He didn't like that much either, but retired early to write his best books: a History of England which was strong on the governmental, institutional side, and a History of the Royal College of Physicians. He had a real interest in science and medicine.

He often used to come up to my rooms to chat, and was a fascinating talker, full of ideas and bubbling over with fun. None of this got into his writing, which was a pity: he had been schooled in the impersonal manner of Firth. Trevelyan came over to consult Firth's fine collection of seventeenth-century pamphlets and broadsides. Firth said, 'You interested in writing about these old people?' Trevelyan said, 'Yes, of course: aren't you?' Firth replied, 'No: only reading them.'

G.N. bustled up one day. 'You must be in this morning,

for the Master of Trinity is here and wants specially to see you.' When Trevelyan appeared he said: 'You are engaged on a really big book, as few are. I want you to stick to it, and not turn aside.' Much impressed – he wasted no words – I thought, goodness, if that's what he thinks I *must* get forward with my portrait of the England of Elizabeth. He was an encourager, as great men are apt to be, not a discourager, as the inferior like to be. Later, when I got to know him and became his friend, he said: 'We thought that you were never going to begin, but once started, there's no stopping you.'

Well, I had to make up for lost time, wasting time on the People. I now know that I could not have borne it, in any capacity, in any form or occupation. The way was now clear for me to concentrate on my true vocation. Fortunately, in all my divagations I had never ceased to write, and happily I had a large fund of materials accumulated upon which to go forward.

✻

One of the most promising of our elections was the young Christopher Hill. Sumner may have advised him in the same sense, but I urged that Russia was the most important subject to get into for the future. Perhaps Christopher saw it for himself: he took up Russian, went to the USSR – and came back a converted Communist. This was a bit much.

I had had trouble in this field before. My friend Ralph Fox of Magdalen was a prominent figure in the Communist Party. He was their best specimen as a writer, their foremost intellectual, after the absurd Palme Dutt of Balliol, whose spectrum of the world was upside down: half-Swede, half-Indian, he should have confined his attentions to Swedish India.

Ralph Fox was a more serious proposition. We used to

have fierce arguments, for he took the Stalinist line that the Social Democrats in Germany were 'social fascists'. He refused to see the absolute necessity of the Communists pulling together with the Socialists, the unity of the working-class movement, if Germany were to be saved from Hitler. From the in-fighting of Communists against Socialists, it would not be the Communists who would win, but the Nazis. Hitler, who had an acute sense of power, could bank on that. My argument all through that disastrous decade was that the Left forces, the only hope of international peace, were everywhere without any sense of power. In 1932 the Communists actually joined with the Nazis in the Berlin Tram Strike, directed against the Socialist administration in Prussia.

Eventually facts broke down Ralph Fox's doctrinaire convictions and, disillusioned, he asked me if I couldn't find him a footing in Oxford. Nothing doing at Magdalen. And I had no luck with canny Warden Adams, any more than I had when I suggested Bertrand Russell, then out of a job, for a Research Fellowship. Ralph was ordered by the Party to Spain, where he was shot down on the Cordoba Front by German war planes.

Christopher Hill had something in common with Ralph – I think both Yorkshiremen: they had a feminine cast of mind, which looked for authority to direct them, instead of thinking things out for themselves. That is what half my inner struggle had been about. Christopher's parents were ardent Nonconformists, with a missionary streak, and – my goodness – he became a missionary for Communism and, when that caved in, for the revolutionary Puritans (equally intolerable and intolerant) of the seventeenth century. His enlightenment about Communism did not take place until 1956, with the attack on Hungary. Fancy not having seen the light with Stalin's appalling purges of the comrades years before in the Thirties!

My principle in editing my series was to recruit a writer

sympathetic to the subject, not someone who would sabotage it. When I gave a young provincial academic the opportunity to write a volume on Drake, he treated the greatest navigator of his time as merely a pirate. Not good enough. When Christopher turned in his book on Lenin and the Russian Revolution I got another surprise. It was not merely orthodox Stalinism, but wholly impersonal, not a human touch. I suggested a few to humanise it – for instance, Lenin on top of a bus showing Trotsky around London and, with a dismissive gesture: 'That's *their* Westminster Abbey.' He meant, not of the English people, but of the capitalist bourgeoisie.

Because of its subject at that time Christopher's was the most successful biography in the series. I acquired some blame for it in USA, little as I liked the book. Years later I asked him if he wouldn't revise it. 'No: sick of the subject', and indeed no wonder! But he has not yet got sick of his dear Puritans, though he has revised himself a little there too.

A most original book in the series was K.B. McFarlane's *Wyclif*, full of completely new information from manuscript sources. One had to be very careful with him, for he would do only what he liked on his own terms, and suggested his own subject. Then he wouldn't have the obvious title, Wyclif and the Reformation, but the cumbrous *Wyclif and the Beginnings of English Nonconformity*. He found out much that was new about the Lollards, but insisted that they had nothing to do with the Reformation. The great authority was wrong, for the Lollards were being persecuted by Wolsey right up to the threshold of the Reformation and linked up with it. However, this was the only book that McFarlane ever wrote. He was one of those who couldn't get their books written, and had an acute psychosis about those who could.

My friend in College, G.F. Hudson, was another. Intellectually, he was more remarkable, one of the few whom I held as a mentor. He had an ecumenical spread of mind. He knew about the Far East, China and Japan: for College research he was supposed to be writing about the Tokugawa epoch. He never got round to it. He knew the Middle East, from early archaeological work under Stanley Casson in Constantinople. He knew about the interior of Tibet and that of Tammany Hall; American politics as well as Russian; also South America. It amused me that, when a boy at Plymouth, he was the only boy in the school who didn't know who the reigning mayor of Plymouth was, and the only one who knew who was the conqueror of Adrianople at the time.

Toynbee, in writing his world-famous *Study of History*, consulted Hudson. Geoffrey replied with a few paragraphs, in the footnotes, which completely blew the whole Challenge-and-Response theme of the book. Toynbee did not seem to notice – a 'rubbery man' Richard Pares called him and devoted a serious analysis of the book to articles in the *English Historical Review*, of which he was editor, in succession to Clark. Trevor-Roper merely made fun of it. When I read his flippant article in *Encounter* to Trevelyan, the great man was irritated by it. He was not amused. 'But what does he say that is positive? What does he think?' he kept asking. Nothing constructive could be extracted, to Trevelyan's displeasure and my amusement.

Sumner was getting more and more ill, and often in bed. He was to do the volume on Peter the Great for me. Here was a job he could do without having to go out to libraries. He was grateful, and wrote a good authoritative book. An absurd query about a word showed him in a characteristic light. The Russian Bear's habits were notoriously uncouth: could Humphry dare to say that in public he farted? There was a to-do about this: Humphry faltered and paltered. Of course he could use Strachey's meiosis and say, as he had of some Elizabethan before the Queen, bending low 'he gave vent to an unfortunate sound'. Humphry summoned up all his courage, poor fellow, and settled it bravely that Peter the Great farted.

One of the best things Sumner did as Warden was to take advantage of Craster's retirement from being Bodley's Librarian to make him ours. He turned out to be a very live wire, and in his quiet way he had drive. At the Bodleian he had proved a reformer. It fell to him to organise the big new Bodleian, which he had not been responsible for building – Giles Scott's monstrous erection uglifying that end of Broad Street. Craster had favoured a totally new Bodleian on the available site in Holywell. The conservative spirit of this scion of a very ancient stock turned out to be more open-minded and flexible than the conventional liberals. His idiosyncratic features are recorded in a gargoyle on a cornice in the Old Schools Quadrangle. When Lady Craster asked Lady Powicke what she thought of it, the latter only just refrained from saying: 'Just like an old gargoyle.'

For the Codrington Craster did a fine job, after Oman's long soporific reign. During that we made a horrid mistake. With shelves overloaded we had a space-problem. We decided to unload shelves of extinct theology, Bampton Lectures and such. We made a present of our surplus books to the Brotherton Library at Sheffield. Among the earlier books were very valuable works on early science, including a first edition of Newton's *Principia* and other rarities! I was on the Library Committee at the time, as I continued to be throughout most of my time in College; but in those early days I did not appreciate what was happening.

Warden Adams was reluctant to our getting rid of Max Müller's Oriental musings – were they *Chips from a German Workshop*? However, he never resented being over-ridden, and took it all in good part. Max Müller had been an odd acquisition for the Victorian Fellows to make. He was a gifted pianist among other things, a successful socialite well able to solace the ladies at evening parties at Blenheim. The Bismarckian Mommsen pronounced his epitaph: 'Haf you no hombogs of your own that you must import them from Gairmany?'

Craster solved our problem. At the back of the Codrington he built on an annexe compact with metal shelving. Interested only in the contents of books, I am no expert in librarianship, so I did not appreciate Craster's next reform, the re-numbering of books according to an up-to-date system of mobility. For me it merely meant that I could no longer go down and at any time put my hand familiarly on a book on the shelf where I had long known it to live. However, Progess! One must move with the times, however inconvenient.

Sumner may also have been responsible for the appointment of a new young manciple, Bert Watson. He had been trained under that uncongenial piece of old Balmorality, Wright. I remember Watson as a cherubic, pink-faced scout-boy standing shyly at attention at the smoking-room door when called, cheerful and obliging. He came from a very good Oxford family, and during the war served in the Oxford and Bucks. I kept in touch with him, writing the College news. When he came back to us he qualified as a clerk of works, and inspected all the College roofs, as one-legged Wharton had not been able to do. Watson discovered that the great beam in the roof of the Codrington was hanging at both ends, and in a matter of months the whole ceiling might have collapsed.

After the war years everything everywhere was in need of repair, and under the energetic and thoroughly qualified new manciple a programme of new stonework, re-roofing and re-building was begun, which went on for the next twenty years. I used to wonder whether it needed to take so long. Then I remembered Hardy's professional reflection in *Jude the Obscure* that families of Oxford masons had lived for generations off the buildings. The head-mason in charge was an accomplished craftsman, and his wife became my typist. We made friends, and they regularly came down to stay with me in Cornwall, as did Bert Watson and his wife.

It was fortunate that All Souls had the means to finance all this renewal, and also to help other colleges with their dilapidations. Otherwise this was a bleak time – the country hardly recovered breath until 1952, the young Elizabeth II's accession. Austerity was not only the rule but a prime necessity. Sumner hardly ever entertained a guest, except an occasional academic, like Professor Dover Wilson from Edinburgh. Humphry was afraid that we might not agree about Shakespeare and the Elizabethans. He was afraid about everything. Actually Dover and I got on very well; I liked his enthusiasm, though knowing how erratic the Eng. Lit. professor was apt to be. (It made his edition of Shakespeare's Sonnets valueless.)[1]

❋

The time had come for me to make the acquaintance of America – belatedly. Reggie Harris and Richard Pares had been able to go over when young, with the aid of Rockefeller grants. I was now awarded one, to visit the Huntington Library in California, lecture and get an idea of its rich resources for research. Humphry as ever was kind and 'caring', as the cliché goes today. He was anxious lest I 'missed my footing', and typically added that the ship's hooter sounding over the waste of waters in mid-Atlantic was the most desolate sound he knew. That was hardly cheering, and I never liked those trans-Atlantic crossings, though I was to make many, by sea and by air (Oman and I had agreed that we would never travel by air).

By seniority I was now Sub-Warden, my one idea to stand (or, rather, sit) by the Warden and help him in every respect. Owing to the war and the long intermission of

---

[1] See my *Discovering Shakespeare*, 26-7.

elections our ranks were depleted, and Sumner favoured four a year, instead of the usual two. Perhaps he thought that this would be more popular in the university – he had a Balliol point of view. When he was absent, ill, it fell to me to preside over College meetings. Twice I had to propose these double numbers. Numbers three and four in the list were not necessarily below the level of numbers one or two. However, they would not have been elected without my advocacy; whether I wished it or not, I fell in with the Warden's wishes. Isaiah said blithely of one philosopher: 'He's mad, but he may be a genius.' We took the risk – and what a confounded nuisance he was.

This led to a strong afforcement of juniors, and at the core of them were Isaiah's '*sans-culottes*', a group of pre-hippies who worried Humphry no end. He could not control them and, a sick man, wanting to do his best for them, he was afraid of them. They did not consider him in the least. One of these advanced specimens had a mistress in London. When she threw him out, he had to burgle her flat to retrieve his passport and wallet. It happened to be his duty to attend the university sermon at St Mary's at 10 a.m. on Sunday. After an all-night party in London he would charter a taxi to bring him back to Oxford in time. Think of the expense! He didn't.

One episode he thought comic. Having married, he thought it would make a good gesture to the Warden to ask him to lunch at the newly-weds' love-nest in Oxford. Humphry arrived and, while the lunch was cooking, so did the gas-man. The Fellow had no cash for the meter to complete cooking the meal: he had to borrow it from the Warden. I do not think Humphry was amused, but the young man thought it made a good story to tell. Before he became a Fellow he had rather made up to me. I warned him that people would take him at his own valuation. He did not agree: his cue was to amuse them, and perhaps he was right. Nor was my line popular with the group.

Perhaps they thought it patronising; but if it had not been for my advocacy, or patronage in the case of my pupil John Cooper, half of the group would not have been elected.

Humphry had a lot to put up with from them – what a contrast it was with the old stately ways! Though I had been a Leftist when young I respected and liked the senior Fellows, regarded some of them with affection, especially Oman and Robertson. And how much one learned from them, from their knowledge and experience! Not so this new generation: they had nothing to learn from the senior Fellows. Notably the psychotic Cooper, who would not even address them.

I did not know one half of the story, for I was on a second visit to America. But at Humphry's last College meeting there was Cooper slanging the Warden, and the Warden shouting back at him. Unthinkable in the old gentlemanly days, and especially with Humphry, who was above all a gentleman, too much so for dealing with them. He went into hospital for a duodenal operation, and shortly died. His last words were: 'Tell the junior Fellows that I am thinking of their problems.'

CHAPTER 6

Crisis – Hiatus

Suddenly we were faced with the unexpected problem of finding a Warden. In Pember's time it had been generally assumed that Chelmsford would succeed him. When Chelmsford suddenly died there was a Sub-Warden available, and Adams was elected. The general assumption now was that Edward Bridges would accept the job. He would have made a very powerful Warden indeed.

The son of the famous Poet Laureate, he was not much like him, except for his monumental integrity: no aesthete. After service in the 1914-1918 War he went into the civil service and became a great servant of the state. There was something of greatness about him, and Hancock observed how much the country owed to him in winning the war. As Secretary to the Cabinet, after work all day he took home more papers to work on until midnight year after year. Every morning there would be the business ready, in order of priority for decisions to be made by Churchill and Cabinet. His efficiency was exemplary.

In Germany everything depended on the inspiration of the divine Führer, often erratic. It is consoling to think that our conduct of the war at the top was actually more *efficient* than Germany's. Not many people would have expected that, and Bridges was uncommunicative. I shared rooms with him for a time, and whenever he passed through mine he always found me at work on my book at my heavily laden table, notes, manuscripts, books in order. He

155

approved, rather warmly for him. So I dared to tease him about all the secrets of state in that ice-cold mind. 'Yes, and they will remain in the deep, deep fridge.' One day he did ask me how Elizabeth I arrived at her decisions. I told him that she always hesitated, pondered and seemed unclear, till almost sub-consciously the decision came clear. He said that this was much like Winston's way. He never spoke of his famous father, except to say one day that he was at present underestimated, Hopkins overestimated, but that time would put that right.

Bridges, who had become Head of the Treasury and the whole Civil Service, was due to retire and would be available for us. No problem. Then Attlee, with whom he was a prime influence, persuaded him to remain on. Things were still critical in Whitehall and in the country: Bridges's experience and clear mind were invaluable. I have often wondered whether it was not he who advised Attlee to make the essential decision to put Bevin at the Foreign Office instead of Dalton who expected the assignment.

Now we were suddenly let down: it was my duty to find a suitable replacement. Eric Beckett of the Foreign Office came to mind. There he was head of the legal department, but with proper liberal sympathies – for me his having been an anti-Chamberlainite was a recommendation. When Eden had left the Foreign Office, I said to Beckett one evening at dinner in Hall, half inquiringly, that Eden had been 'bumped off' by Chamberlain. Beckett replied that it was the Foreign Office that had been bumped off. That night Churchill, who never lost a night's sleep throughout the war, spent a sleepless night. He knew what it meant: Chamberlain was determined on peace with Hitler. Well, it was possible – but on Hitler's terms.

Beckett had immense, even boyish, charm. All this should have recommended him to the Left among the younger generation, but they didn't know him. Hard at work all through the war he had not been much in College,

156

and they all took against him. Cooper circulated the word: 'We hear so much about Beckett's charm, but he has not chosen to shed much of it on the junior Fellows.' Donald Somervell commented peaceably: 'Nor has Cooper shed much of *his* charm on the senior Fellows.' Cooper to me: 'I would a thousand times rather have you for Warden than Beckett.' It was simply prejudice on their part. They were acting collectively as a party, as they had done with Humphry.

And they had a Partei-Führer in Rees – he acted exactly as he did later as Principal at Aberystwyth, making himself leader of the young students there against the Faculty, which brought about his downfall. No question of his co-operating with the other College officers to see us through the emergency. He came up with a candidate from among the young, whom the seniors wouldn't agree to have. We were in a jam. Bob Brand said to me, 'Why don't you take it, Leslie?' I never considered it: I had found a suitable man, a public affairs man – not a lightweight of a young academic put forward by Rees – and I would stand stolidly by my candidate.

Rounding up support for him put paid to the *sans-culottes* and their man, who withdrew from the fight. Crazy Cooper stationed himself day after day, in a deck-chair at the foot of my staircase, to keep an eye on whoever was coming to consult me. They were enraged at their defeat – one could also call them the *enragés*. John Foster thought that I had 'put a fast one across'. Nothing of the sort: it was merely my duty to provide a suitable candidate for Warden. But nothing would induce them to accept him. Some among the seniors, notably Malcolm and Salter, thanked me for delivering the College from an unsuitable choice. The tug-of-war went on. Meeting after meeting took place: no decision.

Meanwhile, I was having to take the Warden's place in College business, all the committees, electoral boards – no help from the estates bursar, who acted as a leader of Opposition all the way through. Having responsibility without authority, I became their chief target. One could now appreciate something of what Humphry had suffered from them, the joys of running such an institution. At an electoral board meeting for our chair of economics Maurice Bowra, then Vice-Chancellor, presided with brisk promptness, said his piece on behalf of Roy Harrod; then left us to be railroaded by the authority on the subject, Lionel Robbins, who pushed in his favourite John Hicks.

Roy's judgment in economic affairs was volatile; Hicks's was not much better, perhaps a shade. I recall the judicious Brand inviting Roy to dinner, using him as a sounding board, rather than a pace-maker. Roy poured out his theories enthusiastically, Brand simply listening – dismissively, Roy didn't seem to be aware. Economics is a *practical* subject.

During this interval I had also to receive the College guests. When Chancellor Adenauer visited Oxford it fell to me to show him round All Souls – the juniors would not join in. Significantly this old German of his generation appreciated only medieval Gothic – no eye for the eighteenth-century classical. Looking round the fifteenth-century front quad he commented: 'Es ist besser als die Politik', probably without sincerity. Photographs were taken of the sly old monkey-face. He was no friend of England. All the same a great man. A Rhinelander, it was much to his credit that he was not an admirer of the Prussian Bismarck and the policy of 'blood and iron', with which he welded modern Germany.

My former American pupil from Merton was now on the American staff, one of the first people to penetrate the horrors of Belsen. (An Oxfordshire MP, Sir Archibald Southby, died from the germ he picked up there.) My pupil, now a brigadier, brought to my rooms a representative group of Germans, one of the first lot to be brought out of their claustrophobic nightmare. Their leader, the elderly head of the Technical High School in Munich, thought that, since Germany had prospered under Bismarck, nothing could be said against him. No idea that Bismarck had killed representative government, created a régime deliberately not responsible to the electorate, and collected enemies for Germany by his bullying and thrusting aggression. Here was the typical German. As they left my rooms a younger man drew me aside to say that he knew what I meant, and agreed. He was from Hamburg, the civilised margin of the interior morass.

Since there was no majority for Beckett a compromise candidate was put up. This was Hubert Henderson. He would have been a satisfactory Warden if he had been well. A Cambridge man, he had had a great deal of experience of public life in London. An economist, he was yet a practical Scot, of good judgment. After the erosion of the country's resources in the war, Keynes, optimistic as ever, advocated the maximum expenditure on social services, the consumer society. Henderson advocated the minimum, and he was right. Austerity in consuming, hard work in producing was the right way to rebuild our resources.

It was not an agreeable choice, for Henderson had a bad heart-condition, in fact was fatally affected. When his election was announced to him in the smoking-room he trembled all over like a leaf. To make his entry upon the Lodgings easy, I got the College to take over carpets and curtains, and fuelling; there was a fuel shortage. The Lodgings already contained some historic pieces, portraits and fine Georgian mirrors, etc. Henderson entered them only once, and then could not mount the stairs.

The next thing was Encaenia. I was in the big quad to receive guests, when my old tutor, Masterman, ran up to tell me that the Warden had had a stroke during the proceedings in the Sheldonian, and that I must take charge. Emergency — even Cooper rallied to help. I told him

159

to look after Edith Evans, among the honorands, while I received M. Antonin Besse, who had just founded St Antony's College, and Vincent Auriol, the admirable Socialist President of the French Republic. I do not remember all the others. Luncheon was in the Hall, on a smaller scale, not in the great Codrington Library – our resources as yet did not run to that. At Cliveden that weekend Nancy Astor said, 'I heard you were very grand at All Souls.' Nonsense: I was merely doing my bit, standing in the breach.

Actually, my situation was worse than before: I still had to conduct affairs on the spot, without authority, and having to go between the College and a sick Warden up in North Oxford who never came into residence. It was a ghastly time – how frustrating may be seen from the fact that all that year I wrote not a word of my own research book. All I could do was, in the intervals of interruptions, to go on with my translation of Lucien Romier's *History of France*. I did my bit at entertaining guests: Raymond Carr described me as the 'châtelaine' of All Souls. No one guessed what a bore I found it.

A rather equivocal case was that of André Maurois's first visit to Oxford after the war. He had made a bad mistake in New York at the fall of France. The prime French authority on Britain, who had made his career writing about us, he attacked Britain. A fellow-Jew gave him two hard slaps, 'un comme français, un comme juif'. Churchill, with his gift of phrase, said: 'We thought we had a friend, but found we had only a client.' The sensitive Seznec was on tenter-hooks as to how I should receive Maurois (his real name was Herzog), who after the war had been excluded from our Embassy in Paris. Seznec need not have worried: Maurois had been kind to my first programmatic little book, *On History*, and a Celt does not forget a good turn. I decided that he had simply lost his nerve in New York and panicked – he hadn't needed to say anything, he could just

160

have shut up. So I gave him a good welcome, and we became regular friends.

Thereupon Ava Waverley took it upon her to protest: 'I hear that you were very kind to Maurois at Oxford.' What had it got to do with her? She was a friend too but, bilingual, regarded French affairs as *her* province. She herself was a controversial figure, a target for jokes. When she captured Sir John Anderson in the food shortage, someone said: 'Was it a *coup de foudre*?' Ava was supposed to have replied: 'No, it was not the *good food*.' Her complexion was remarkably blue; naughty young Alan Pryce Jones said it was that of a 'poisoned meringue'. A Bodley by descent, she always came to Encaenia – to the very end when, in the Codrington, I had practically to carry her to the 'Ladies'.

At College meetings I had no trouble from the *sans-culottes* as Humphry had had: he had been afraid of them. But they continued domestically in their undomestic ways. The 'mad' philosopher would come back at 2 a.m., turn on his bath and sing the Latin Creed at the top of his voice. Next morning the sensitive Seznec would come to me to complain, haggard in the face from a sleepless night next door. I was well away from these amenities, ensconced in my corner a whole quad away. Then this bright spark journeyed all the way across to take a bath in my private bathroom and wipe himself all over in my face-towel. What was the idea? Completely un-house-trained, army service was no excuse for such manners. How unlike the old gentlemanly College of Pember and Anson!

Meanwhile the situation regarding the Warden was intolerable; it was too awkward for me to deal with. Fortunately Simon, who was Senior Fellow, now took it in hand. He wrote a surprising letter to say how pleased he and other seniors were at my having become such 'a pillar of the College'. I did not think in such terms, to me the College was simply my home. I loved it as such and was ready to make any sacrifice for it. Simon clearly loved it too, but could not express it himself. One Gaudy night he took me by surprise at dessert in the Common Room by reciting the whole two paragraphs at the end of the essay I had written about the nature of All Souls in a recent book, *The English Past*. It was a purple passage, a kind of evocation. What a memory he had!

He set himself to clarify poor Henderson's situation, which no one had been able to do. He could not bring himself to resign; perhaps he was too ill to make up his mind. Rees and Company suspected that I was trying to force him out. Nothing of the kind: I was waiting upon events, the doctors gave no hope of his recovery. Simon's resolution was surprising; he went up to see Henderson and came back with the resignation in his pocket.

The way was open for a fresh election. Pressure was put upon me to let my name go forward; senior Fellows, College officers like Craster, evidently Simon himself (though he did not come into the open) wanted me to stand. College loyalty more than anything made me consent, though in my heart I did not want it. A letter from Archibald confirmed my doubt. He wrote: 'You must not take it on. For the first year or two you might find it interesting. After that you would find it a prison. Your vocation is to write – and not turn aside.' I knew that he was right, and only then understood why successive Wardens had always listened to the advice of this quiet, unassuming Canadian lawyer. I was torn in two, for could I let down the good friends who had stood by me all through this testing hiatus in the College?

Loyalty is sometimes a mistake. I had loyally allowed my name to go forward at Christ Church, of which I had been so proud to be a Scholar – to be turned down. In Penryn and Falmouth my Labour Party officers had pressed me to stand again after doing well in the hopeless *débacle* of 1931. I stood again and came nearer to winning – as I

would have done next time. There was to be no next time.
And neither rejection had been forgiven.

In College the younger generation came up with a
candidate of their own, who had enough support among the
seniors, especially among the lawyers, to enable him to
win. This was John Sparrow. He had the prime
recommendation of being one of the boys. He was frank and
friendly with them, would open his mind to them about his
career. Should he stick to the Bar, and the London life he so
much enjoyed? – he was very clubbable. Should he put in
for the librarianship of the Bodleian? (He would have been
good at that.) Or should he – Humphry's *bête noire* – put in
for Warden? It would never have occurred to me to discuss
my future with any of them. And Rees told me that a prime
objection of the younger Fellows was that *they did not know
me*.

This was another surprise. Could he honestly say that he
did not know me? He answered that he thought he did. And
added that he thought I was '*strong* – terribly strong'. They
all thought that I 'wanted to run the place'. Later they
found that this was far from the case – no allowance made
for standing in the breach and taking the rap in distressing
circumstances, with no help from them – above all,
sacrificing what I cared for most, my writing. Truly enough,
they did not know the real me – Rees was right enough
about that.

In spite of the support of a few close friends it was a
lonely time, faced by a coherent, organised opposition. In
London Rees could organise support for his candidate; in
College Lionel Butler was assigned the job of whipper-in.
The result was not in doubt, though Cole said to me: 'Don't
withdraw now.' When Simon saw which way the majority
lay he went over to the other side – understandably, for he
was conducting the election and had to produce a decision.

Quite apart from my own interest in the matter, I did not
want Sparrow for Warden. We had never been very

friendly, and I thought him a light-weight. Wilberforce was a heavier weight, but no one thought of him. He might have made an obvious choice if he had taken on the estates bursarship as I had wished – and there was a clear Wykehamist majority among us. The result was in the bag, and I had to declare it in Chapel.

Meeting John in the Law reading-room of the Codrington I said there were two things that pleased me about the Election. It would give pleasure to his mother. (She was a charming woman: the whole family had a complex against the father, who was pernickety and difficult.) Secondly, he had an undoubted majority, always awkward when it is a near thing. It gave me an alibi. No one knew how that would work out. Cyril Falls, distressed at the result, said: 'But you will always remain influential in the College.' That was precisely what I intended not. They could look after their own affairs: I would confine myself to my own. When I told Rees that I should disinterest myself from the College, he said kindly: 'Don't disinterest yourself too much.' He had won. He did not know my resolve and how ironically things would work out – a bitter blow from others became an almighty stroke of luck for me.

That evening it fell to me to propose the health of the new Warden. I said that, after so much ill health with our Wardens, he did not know how fortunate he was never to have had a day's illness in his life. 'But – *long may it continue!*' It did.

❖

My term of office was coming to an end – an historical hiatus in the record of the College: John would sometimes address me as Sub-Warden by mistake after I had ceased. Simon wanted to propose a formal resolution of thanks from the whole College. I quashed that: I had merely done my duty for the institution I loved, and wanted nothing more from

164

them. Before my term ended and I packed up, Rees came to say that he was giving up the bursarship: he had been offered the principalship of Aberystwyth College. He gave every reason for accepting it: good salary, official house, good climate, good schooling for the children. All these were secondary reasons. I was longing to get rid of him, but treated him honestly and put the prime question he had ignored: 'Do you think you will be able to stand it?' He did not answer this: the event showed that he could not.

He had been put across that institution, against the wishes of the Faculty who had a better candidate, by Tom Jones, a kind of uncrowned king in Wales, immensely public-spirited and influential. T.J., as we all called him, was a friend of Lionel Curtis, and was stuck on All Souls. I saw him there from time to time and also at Cliveden, and liked him. These two Celts got on well. But I never knew what a snake in the grass he was about Appeasement. Celtic intuition told him never to mention the subject to me. He was in fact one of the most active of the gang making up to Hitler. As former Secretary to Lloyd George, then Baldwin, he was able to bring pressure on them to go to the footstool at Berchtesgaden and kiss the foot of the divine Führer. He got Lloyd George to go, be flattered and make a fool of himself. He could not persuade Baldwin – too indolent, and too uninterested in foreign affairs!

At Aberystwyth the new Principal acted, as he had done in College, as a Partei-Führer, popular with the students, with whom he made common cause and played football – disrespected by the Faculty. Warm-hearted – and perhaps making up to me – he invited me over to give some Elizabethan lectures. I gladly accepted, for I wanted to consult Welsh historians for the most difficult chapter, on Wales, for my research-work 'The Expansion of Elizabethan England'. It offered a chance to do some research into the Godolphin manuscipts in the admirably empty National Library of Wales. (It should have been at Cardiff.)

I enjoyed my visit. It made no difference to my opinion of Goronwy: I had taken his measure long ago. There shortly followed the catastrophe which confirmed it. There broke upon the country the thunderclap of Burgess and Maclean's escape to Moscow and their revelation as spies for the KGB. They were friends of Rees's. He now made a characteristic mistake. As usual he was in debt, and for £2,000 he wrote a couple of articles for *The People* giving his version of the affair. Another motive may have been to exculpate himself, and he was frightened. What I thought caddish was that, though he knew about Anthony Blunt, he did not mention him but gave away the name of his working-class friend. The articles made a great hullabaloo, and gave Aberystwyth the chance to get rid of him. Goronwy was ostracised by all his Oxford friends. Maurice Bowra wrote to him that the campus at Aberystwyth should be sown with Judas-trees. Rees did not dare to show his face again at All Souls and, when at length he did, I did not speak to him.

The first half of his career had been all good luck, he had the knack of falling on his feet; the second half was all bad luck – unduly, unfairly. His life was broken in two, and made a curious case. Years before, Elizabeth Bowen put a caricature of him into *Death of the Heart*. I recognised it at once and said, under my mistake of thinking him a fellow-proletarian: 'This is what you get by giving yourself away to the upper classes. Why don't you give it up, shut yourself up for five or ten years and write a 'Tudor Wales', like my *Tudor Cornwall*. It is a wonderful subject.' He answered candidly, 'My dear Leslie, I couldn't do it.'

That was it: he hadn't the character to make himself do it. He could have done it: he had the talents for it; he wrote well and even knew Welsh. What a pity – for it *is* a wonderful subject, and the Welsh academics had written only bits and pieces of it, never a synoptic work, if on a smaller scale, like *Tudor Cornwall*.

CHAPTER 7

Warden Sparrow

Sparrow's election was the beginning of a long euphoria. The young men had got their man, and were appeased. For me it was an almighty deliverance. I did not want to spend my life on committees deciding who should cook, or cook up, what. John enjoyed committees and didn't mind the waste of time. Raymond Carr wrote recently that I should have 'blessed' the young men for my deliverance. Every one of them junior to Rohan Butler, our last election before the War, had voted against me, though I had been responsible for the election of half of them, or at least a quarter.

Should I have been grateful? It all worked out far better and more comfortably than I could ever have expected. Still, I knew well enough what their motive had been – summed up in the neat slogan, 'Stop Rowse!' I had had enough of that all along, and decided on a policy – never to put myself again in any position where I depended on others. I could always answer for myself, make myself do what I meant to do. Whenever I depended on others ... I remembered my friend in Cornwall, Bertie Abdy. His wife heard him say, at a lunch party of hers: 'Je déteste les autres.'

Fortunately some of 'les jeunes' began to hive off to teaching jobs in other colleges. Cooper, who had been such a nuisance to Humphry and to me, went off, as I have said, to Trinity. I ceased to recognise him. There must have been something wrong with him, for he died in his forties, his

167

work unaccomplished – and he was an excellent scholar. I forget about the others, for I closed down on them – a clear saving of time at last. I could now shut myself up and concentrate on my own work.

Sparrow settled agreeably into the Lodgings. With his taste, his books and collection of water-colours, he made the rooms more beautiful than they had ever been. For a house-warming present I gave him a Georgian mahogany tripod table. He took a resolution to remove his living quarters upstairs, turning the two best bedrooms, with their view out over his garden, into a kind of flat. He never occupied the gloomy Victorian study downstairs, where one saw successive Wardens at their desk in the only corner where there was any light – Sumner, for example, writing at our time of day, with a quill-pen! John called it the 'Mausoleum', and said that he used the place 'to sack the Fellows'. As Isaiah said, he was 'very sure-footed'.

This shortly became clear over an important issue, his first test. It became the turn of All Souls, according to the rota, to provide the Vice-Chancellor for his period of three years, and it was important for the standing of the College in the university that we should. It had been a good argument for John's election that we should have a Warden, young and enjoying first-class health, to take up his duty. He refused outright. Halifax, as Chancellor, wrestled with him; Salter, my friend – who had supported him, with not a word to me – was shocked. When I heard about it in America I admired John's courage. I should never have dared not to do my duty, and should have died under the strain, as our neighbour, Alec Smith, Warden of New College, had done.

Perhaps John was right: he knew what he was capable of, and what not. His intimate friend Maurice Bowra advised him against, even threatened that he would resign from Council if John took it on. The fact was that he had no time-sense, and little interest in university affairs, in which he never figured. The Bodleian, yes – there he was interested and, an accomplished book-collector and bibliophile, had something to contribute.

It is not unfair to say that, in giving up the Bar (he was never awarded 'Silk') and his agreeable London life for Oxford, he meant to have a good time. He told me later that, on coming back, College business took only two hours a day; by the end of his time, with the developments that took place and the increasing pressure on All Souls to play a bigger part with its resources, it became quite 'hard work'. He hadn't bargained for that.

No doubt he had made some sacrifice in giving up the freedom of London, and occasionally felt his imprisonment. The beautiful Queen Anne house, which Dr Clarke had built for himself on the High Street and then left to the College, had a little the air of a cage. Going out with his young friends after dinner for a night on the town, he would ask, would I take his place in Common Room? Of course I would. Once, there at the head of the long mahogany table, loaded with fruit, wine, silver, snuff-boxes, great silver candelabra making pools of light, he said to me, 'I could drink myself under the table.'

He might have preferred the freedom of a country gentleman's life, for he took to riding out at Wantage with Penelope Betjeman, a devoted horse-woman. He hadn't the figure for it, and frequently fell off, picked himself up again and went on. He had plenty of spirit. He may even have played a game of football occasionally, and followed his favourite Wolverhampton club around their country matches.

We had not been very friendly, and I had an early show-down with him. When my *Expansion of Elizabethan England* came out I got a remarkable letter from his mentor, Cyril Radcliffe, quite out of the blue, for he had ceased to come to College, in fact developed a scunner against it. Unexpectedly, that very critical spirit praised the book highly. (So did the wife of another of John's friends, Vita Sackville-West.) I showed him Cyril's letter, and said: 'Now that you are responsible for this institution just remember that my research books are a first-line of defence for it.' The clever man that he was took the point at once. He completely changed gear and became my best supporter in College. We became friends – in the last years, when I came back from the Huntington Library, practically buddies. We were both cast out of the old All Souls mould, agreed about the College and saw eye-to-eye about the deplorable way things were going. We should not have found a point of disagreement even if we had tried.

The Huntington Library made me an offer of regular visits as a Research Associate, they even offered me permanent tenure. Should I become an expatriate, as several of my literary friends had become, and an increasing number of academics, join the 'brain-drain'? I was tempted for, with my books increasingly successful, I was skinned by penal taxation – for causes I disapproved of and people I detested: incessantly striking trade-unionists, wrecking their own show, silly rioting students for whom everything was done (as it had not been in my case).

The Huntington Library had everything to recommend it. Founded to study the English Renaissance, it had the advantages of both History and English Literature together on the open bookshelves. Just what I wanted – most convenient. Here was a New World to learn, a happy group of new friends, none of the bitter memories of the old. Solitude, concentration on work, I was happy there.

But I could not give up my life at Oxford or in Cornwall. John made no objection to the ambivalent course I followed: a winter of research and writing in California, spring and autumn at All Souls, summer at home in Cornwall. I settled for a half-time Fellowship financially, to be free to do better in America: no need to scrounge for marriage and children's allowances, travel allowances or for books which one then annexed to one's own library. All worked out in the happiest way for work, for I was working wherever I was. As Shakespeare says, you receive a bad blow – and it turns out to be nothing but good. In the end things had turned out for the best. True, I was lonely in America – the old friendly life in College was over; all that was past. Loneliness was good for work and for poetry, always my consolation.

❖

I was lucky also to miss out on the country's downward plunge after Suez, the age of Harold Wilson and Dick Crossman – 'Double Crossman', as Bowra called him (no friend to All Souls) – of rioting students occupying university premises, holding up lectures and examinations. At Essex university, where Rohan Butler was on the governing body, the students did £30,000 worth of direct damage, the indirect cost ten times as much.[1] In Paris the followers of Silly Sartre brought down a great man, De Gaulle, who had resuscitated a broken France. In Oxford students from Ruskin College and the Polytechnic occupied the Examination Schools for days; the mess they made took a fortnight to clear up.

Warden Sparrow made himself a popular, or rather unpopular, target by his outspokenness about all this. Walls sported graffiti reflecting on him, even his private life, not all of them as amusing as that I saw in New College Lane: 'Donate your don to Oxfam.' At one time there was a threat to occupy All Souls and, since the place was full for College meeting, the Warden had the gates closed and barred.

Unexpectedly I had a confrontation with a mob

---

[1] The students had a grievance in untoward, unworkable buildings, following the blueprint of the 'progressive' Noel (Lord) Annan, which he later regretted.

threatening to invade us, carrying their banners, 'Who killed Cock-Sparrow?', etc. There they were, the young fools, congregated on the pavement outside the gate on the High. Since the affair got into the newspapers, and I am the only one to tell what happened, I may as well tell it. Quite used from old days to prating at street-corners, I addressed them. 'What are you doing here, wasting your time when you should be getting on with your work?' 'What about *your* work?', said one of them. That gave me a lead. I said: 'When I was a working-class boy there was only one university scholarship for the whole of my county. I had to get it, or go under.' They had never set eyes on me before; and they listened. Evidently impressed, one of them piped up weakly: 'What about the others?' 'To become a Fellow of All Souls you have to work hard and pass a stiff examination – no question of privilege.' I took the offensive. 'Now, look at you – well-dressed, middle-class young fellows, swaddled in grants, everything done for you – you should be *ashamed* of yourselves!'

I think they were, for with no trouble at all they somewhat shamefacedly sheered off. They had behaved so well to me that, secretly, I would have liked to ask them all in to tea. Impossible – too many, and anyway the College was closed. Tomorrow, I would be off to America: they didn't know that.

Here I am not ashamed to boast that, with all my audiences, in England or America, in those disturbed days or later, I never once had an unfriendly audience, or any opposition. What they responded to was straight talk, they could tell what was sincere, even when it went counter to what was popular. Sparrow made the mistake of compromising with them, going half-way to meet them – 'I rather sympathise with your point of view', etc. This did not really go down with them.

It was not insincere on his part. I used to defend him, and explain that he was not a reactionary, but genuinely and

7. Warden Sparrow

intellectually a liberal. What he feared was that they would bring about a backlash on themselves. Myself, I was not, had never been, a liberal, and would have no objection to a backlash that was salutary and overdue. John really was a kind of old-fashioned Whig, rather like Warden Pember. Like him he was at his best at entertaining, and that was what he liked best, along with book-collecting. His guests were apt to be literary and, when they were, he usually included me. There was ancient Somerset Maugham with his young friend Alan Searle, who looked after him. John put them in a twin-bedded room: 'I think that, at his age, that is *all right*?' Thank heaven, he wasn't a bit 'square', or repressed like poor Humphry Sumner. After lunch we sat in the garden under the chestnut trees. Maugham was so old that he remembered Wilde, said that Oscar had a sweet nature, was totally unmalicious, and all the trouble had come from the malign Lord Alfred. David Cecil was present, and most unsympathetic: Wilde was a man of forty and should not have given way to a mere adolescent. I could not help feeling myself that Wilde was a fool to be led by the nose – if that was the right word for it – by a mere boy of nineteen.

Then there were the Sitwells, not Osbert and Edith who were my friends, but Sacheverell and wife whom I didn't know. John was a friend of the remarkable traveller, Freya Stark, her fingers loaded with Oriental rings: he used to rent her house at Bergamo for the summer vacations. This led to his friendship with Perosa, the Italian scholar with whom he edited a book of Renaissance Latin Verse, complaining to me how few English there were to go into it. I found Perosa, for an Italian, lugubrious.

John had his literary controversies; he liked controversy, it amused his vacant hours. There was an angry one with Helen Gardner about the dating of John Donne's poems. John had a fine collection of his first editions. I don't know which of the two was right. I rather sympathised with

173

John, in his clash with the American biographer of George Eliot, about identifying Mr Casaubon in *Middlemarch* with Mark Pattison, of whom there were surely traits in the depiction of the character. John knew all about Pattison, and was to have written his biography. He contented himself with going through his papers in the Bodleian. Then Cambridge invited him to give the Clark Lectures. He produced an admirable series, which made a book concise and to the point, which told all we needed to know about Pattison and his views on university education, research and scholarship. My attempt to get the book published in New York failed. I had already given the first Trevelyan Lectures at Cambridge on *The Elizabethans and America*: this did get published over there.

Salter had done a fine job over shipping in USA during the second German war. When he produced a book of essays on his varied experiences in public life I also tried to get that published in New York. But, always the civil servant with the impersonal approach, he did not write interestingly. I had more success with getting my American protégés published in England, three or four books on the Civil War. At the cost of writing Forewords to them, and cutting them down by a third, for they were all too long-winded and the writers could never tell what was relevant and what irrelevant. The same was true with a couple of books by a Huntington colleague, which I managed to shape up for the press. No trouble of that kind with John's spare and shapely writing and elegance of phrase.

As a man of taste he did well with the College buildings, and of course conservatively. We needed to expand our accommodation, with the increasing number of Fellows. No monstrosity in the Warden's garden. He retained the little seventeenth-century manciple's house – like a gabled Cotswold cottage – and the extensions added were in keeping. The original roofs in the Old Quad were of the famous Stonefield slates, and enough of these were recovered for re-roofing. The Lodgings themselves needed thorough repair: John refused to move out, and all the restoration and rebuilding went on around him. He was a man of nerve.

Kenneth Clark was a friend from schoolboy days at Winchester. This encouraged John's interest in the arts. He became a friend of Derek Hill, who painted two portraits of him, one for the College. Reynolds Stone became a friend, and together they produced a beautiful book of Latin inscriptions, of which John gave me a copy. When I wrote my book on Oxford in the History of England I dedicated it to him. Always a phrase-maker, he suggested instead of 'for whom' I might say 'in spite of whom'. Of a junior Fellow marrying: 'Fancy giving up All Souls for one body.' Having an acute sense of adolescent good looks, he collected photographs of the ghastly mixture of long-locked undergraduates and trousered females hard to distinguish, under the caption 'Male and Female created He them'.

Of himself he said: 'One Sparrow does not make a Sumner.' In my view he made a better Warden than poor Humphry. True, Sumner had more standing, and more respect, in the university; but in College we were happier with John: Humphry worried us all, and himself to death. John's rule was easy-going, like Pember's, a policy of taking the line of least resistance. Well, it was a policy, and it worked.

He was very good about the College pictures. He located a couple of portraits of eighteenth-century Fellows, one of them a pretty Tilly Kettle, in whose work I was interested. I had written about him in an early essay, and subsequently bought the fine portrait of a young Scotch acting-Governor of Madras. John resurrected from the cellars beneath the Codrington the fragments of the seventeenth-century ceiling of the Chapel, of interest to art historians, for they were the work of the rare Restoration painter Streeter, who had painted the vast roof of Wren's Sheldonian. Finally John rehabilitated the grand 'Noli me tangere' of Raphael Mengs, for which the College had paid a large sum in Rome in the connoisseur days of the eighteenth century. Sparrow as Warden was in the tradition of connoisseurs like Dr George Clarke. However, *he* had quarrelled with the College, and left his books and famous papers to Worcester College.

John was better instructed in the College pictures than most of us, though several of them used to arrest my attention. I admired most the splendid Lawrence of Sir Charles Vaughan, the Regency diplomat who had a noteworthy career in Spain during the Peninsular War and as ambassador in Washington. His papers are all in the Codrington, and he still awaits his biographer. In later years it often fell to me to conduct American students from Oxford summer schools around the College. It amused them to hear Vaughan's story as ambassador in Washington in Andrew Jackson's days. The President, 'Old Hickory', had as his Egeria the attractive Peggy Eaton, whom the purer ladies would not receive. Sir Charles, as a bachelor, could and did entertain her at his parties. The President averred that she was as chaste as driven snow. Thereupon the free-wheeling Senator Charles Sumner emended Shakespeare's lines to read:

> Age cannot wither, nor custom stale,
> Her infinite *virginity*.

The Senator in fact came over to stay in College as Vaughan's guest. In his letter of thanks he spoke highly of its bachelor amenities – in those Regency, or pre-Victorian, days.

Among other pictures I was drawn to the excellent Highmore of Edward Young, almost our only poet. His idiosyncratic work appealed to the French Surrealists; so in our time he was drafted over to their exhibition in Paris. Did they appreciate his famous couplet on Voltaire? –

> You are so witty, profligate, and thin
> At once we think thee Milton, Death, and Sin.

Something of a satyr in his features appears alarmingly above his clerical garb. One of the foremost of eighteenth-century poets, he received no preferment for his much admired works. However, the College provided for him with its fat living of Welwyn.

Above the dais, presiding over our dinners, were the three Chancellors, Salisbury, Curzon, Halifax. I always regretted these disproportionately large canvases, and yet we have recently added another, of our much loved Quintin Hailsham. I preferred Kit-cat size. I also wished that we had been more original and called in some of the admirable portrait painters earlier this century. As Sub-Warden I got Augustus John to do a drawing of Warden Sumner – alas, one can already see death in the drawn features. But we have John's admirable pencil sketch of T.E. Lawrence.

Robertson told me how Hogarth, the archaeologist, brought the young Lawrence to dine in the days before 1914 when he was little more than a boy. He had toured the Middle East for his *Crusader Castles*.

'And how did you do it?'

'I walked.'

'What did you do when you came to the Tigris?'

'I swam it.'

'By Jove,' said Robertson, as impressed as he was meant to be.

One summer I had a lunch-party on the dais for my Hollywood friend, the distinguished film-director, Rouben Mamoulian. He was the first person to give Greta Garbo a star-part in the film about Queen Christina of Sweden (a favourite with Stalin). Mamoulian had given me a lead with his modernising version of *Hamlet*. At lunch it amused me to place David Cecil beneath the portrait of his famous grandfather. The resemblance of the Cecilian features was striking: the high pale forehead, shapely nose, the long tapering fingers.

In the Lodgings Sparrow had the portraits of his predecessors for company, mostly Georgians; also the connoisseur George Clarke. More remarkable was Bower's mournful portrait of Charles I at his trial. A few copies of this picture were treasured in the households of his most loyal followers. Warden Sheldon was one of the most famous of them. Extruded from the Lodgings by the victorious Puritans, he became Archbishop with the Restoration and presided, with immense energy and ability, over the restoration of the Church. So hard-worked was he that he hadn't even time to come down to the opening of the Sheldonian, which he had donated to the university – our Wren's first architectural commission.

*

After the War there was a very proper demand for the expansion of university education. But under the propulsion of the Robbins Report it went beyond all bounds. The able Principal of Lady Margaret Hall, Lucy Sutherland, said that she always thought the Report 'nonsense'. And when Lionel Robbins and I were doctored together at Exeter, he said to me that he was all in favour of expanding these modern universities *'provided we recognise that they are second-rate'*. There was room for such, but not for all the third-rate institutions, which sprang up like mushrooms. A few, even of these, might be justified, but from the evidence not all. People who have spent their lives in universities know that the number of first-class students is strictly limited. Even those up to the level of a university education is limited, though one should leave a generous

178

margin for late developers, etc.

Now the outcry reached Oxford, and it was a popular cry that All Souls should use up its resources. The College was already contributing more than any other to university funds – even a large sum to Keble's new buildings. (They should join up their front to their Warden's Lodgings, as Butterfield designed, not leave an awkward gap.) Spend-Spend-Spend was all the cry in the Silly Sixties; never think of saving anything for a rainy day, or for the necessities that inevitably arise. When they do, take out a mortgage on the future – such was the general attitude of that post-war generation. It was not in keeping with either Sparrow's or my principles or conduct of our personal affairs. One of the Visiting Fellows concluded, when I told him that I always saved, that my economic views were quite 'out of date'. He left the College owing it several hundred pounds.

How then should All Souls deploy its surplus revenues to the best purpose, in what direction should the College expand? Here Warden Sparrow was at a loss; he was not intimately in touch with these matters. A popular notion was that we should take in undergraduates like all the other colleges. No room where the existing buildings were adequate only for a college of forty Fellows – we had already expanded beyond that limit. Very well: build an undergraduate annexe! Since this was the popular cry Sparrow made the mistake of consenting to it. I took the opportunity of asking the opinion of McFarlane of Magdalen, one of the most experienced tutors in the university, who was thoroughly in touch with its needs. He was firmly of the opinion that undergraduates were already well provided for, and that that was not the way ahead for All Souls. That settled my mind for me.

In the 1930s we had already given hospitality to a number of remarkable figures as 'Associate Members'. Sir Robert Borden, former Prime Minister of Canada, came to deliver some Rhodes lectures. André Siegfried had begun his career with a book on New Zealand, and was regarded as an expert on the British Empire – so far as a Frenchman could be. How puzzled he was to learn that George Lansbury, the Socialist leader, was a devout Anglo-Catholic. Ernest Jacob brought in Gustave Le Bon, a medieval canonist who subsequently became head of the Sorbonne. From Dublin I recruited Myles Dillon, head of the Irish Academy, who wanted to research into the Bodleian's holdings of ancient Celtic manuscripts. Surely this indicated a way ahead, a sphere of usefulness, something different from duplicating undergraduate facilities? Something that was in keeping with the nature of All Souls, and with the tradition of before the War.

Our visitors were usually people involved in public affairs, such as Smuts and Herzog, those rivals, from South Africa: Menzies and his disappointed rival Evatt, from Australia. Lawrence Lowell, President of Harvard, came to explore the folios of Wren's designs in the Codrington for an unused one which might serve for a War Memorial Chapel at Harvard. That lithe and springy old Bostonian walked me off my feet around Christ Church Meadows. André Siegfried became something of a friend. A Republican, he was surprised at my wishing that the July Monarchy had continued, to give constitutional continuity in France, instead of all the chops and changes, the insecurity and disarray right up to our own time.

Sir Robert Borden, war-time Prime Minister of Canada, was an old-fashioned Victorian gentleman: I see him now, with his crinkly hair parted in the middle, his loping stride and yellow boots. He was kind to the highbrow youth that I was, and tried to convert me to the poetry of Archibald Lampman. He certainly knew what was what about Beaverbrook and his reputation on the Montreal Exchange. There was one equivocal public figure who never appeared within our walls.

7. Warden Sparrow

I used to wish that we had more literary visitors. Among the few was Charles Whibley, an early patron of T.S. Eliot. He wrote about the Tory circle of Disraeli, Lord John Manners and Young England. He described to me vividly 'pain of the fifth nerve', an excruciating form of neuralgia, from which Lang also suffered. With him it came from years of overwork: it knocked him out his first year as Archbishop of Canterbury. Then he made a miraculous recovery – not due to Our Lady of Fatima, as with Pope John Paul II, but to two trips around the Mediterranean with Pierpont Morgan. Nor did E.F. Benson have any message for me – I might have been more alert if I had known that one day I should receive his brother A.C. Benson's Medal from the Royal Society of Literature. One week-end Arthur Salter had H.G. Wells for guest. I missed that occasion, made memorable by another guest, a Polish count, monopolising the talk and obliterating Wells with his squeaky voice. However, his famous mistress, Rebecca West, became a good friend and would descend into Oxford from her hilly eyrie up at Ipsden. So also the poet Martyn Skinner, then well known for his *Letters to Malaya*.

Other young writers visited me on their own. Christopher Isherwood only once: a prissy youth, hair parted in the middle like a demure Victorian governess. Stephen Spender brought along his Guardsman, Tony Hyndman, to tea. I saw more of Wystan Auden from my old College, Christ Church, and later kept in touch with him in New York.[2] Archie Campbell was closer to that lot and shared their frolics in rollicking Weimar Germany.

Cyril Connolly came down two or three times. On a first visit the professional egoist was taken up with reading my marginal comments in his *Enemies of Promise*. On a second visit I read him a lecture on the pro-Germanism of the Left

[2] See my *The Poet Auden: A Personal Memoir*.

intellectuals, the group around Kingsley Martin's *New Statesman*. Connolly knew no history but registered the historical argument, which had its proper effect. On another occasion we had tea in our Common Room garden. He was struck by the way the bare branches of the espaliered figtree along the walls looked like the pipes in a ship's engine-room. He certainly had an alert vision and an original way of expressing it, the Irish gift for verbiage.

Among later Associate Members a comic episode was supplied by one Turner, who was to give the Ford Lectures. This old buffer had begun as a protégé of F.W. Maitland, but had nothing to tell us about that scholar of genius about whom one would gladly have heard. Turner's one ewe-lamb in the realm of scholarship had been some volume of esoteric legal documents edited for the Selden Society. At dinner one night he let fall the injudicious remark that he *had* a book which he had allowed to remain in type at the printers for forty years.

He evidently thought to impress us by this feat, or perhaps thought it a joke. I turned on him: 'Do you mean to say that you have held up a printing press for forty years, and never produced the book?' This was not the reception the old boy expected. I can see him now – the parchment cheeks flushing a little, the pince-nez wobbling, eyebrows arching up in alarm, the one hair on bald head standing upright.

After such a revelation of silliness I felt free to ruffle him a bit more, and informed him that the Ford Lectures were the chief public event of the year for the History School. There would be an audience of three or four hundred. The eyebrows shot up further – this was no joke.

I did not attend the first of his Ford lectures, with the usual crowded audience. The lecture of course was totally inaudible. After it the lecturer disappeared for a fortnight to Brighton to recuperate from something like a breakdown. When he came back I did attend his last, or penultimate, lecture. The audience was down to a dozen. Even so, a section of his lecture was missing, and as he nervously shuffled his typescript a sheaf of pages fell to the floor.

For such a type of futility I had no use. But Isaiah Berlin, always amused by the human comedy, could mimic him. The old bachelor loved the bachelor life of our Common Room and, above all, gossip, with a bit of malice in it. 'Now – Woodward,' he would inquire, 'are you hostile?'

He stayed on and on after his Ford Lectures – they never reached the press. What he would have liked was to stay with us for good – and we did give him an extra term of bliss after his ordeal. When he died the old fool left us all his silver.

*

Now Edward Bridges weighed in powerfully, very used to getting his own way in Whitehall and confident of getting it with the College. He was already engaged in doing a manful job for the University in raising money for the buildings everywhere in disrepair from the long neglect of the war years. A decided liberal, Bridges was all in favour of Attlee's Welfare State and helped largely to bring it about. He wanted more undergraduates, and an annexe – all of which would have changed the nature of the College. Within our walls the juniors supported him, led by a young Leftist no better – in fact rather worse – than I had been in the Thirties. They were confident that they would win.

They were in for an unpleasant surprise. Warden Sparrow could give no lead; he was caught between two parties, having made the initial mistake of committing himself, perhaps without thinking it out, to the uncongenial idea of an undergraduate annexe – though of course he didn't like it. The College was saved by a new recruit, not someone *e gremio*, but a sensible sociologist who had come to appreciate the uniqueness of All Souls from residing in it. He devoted all one summer to finding out what each of us thought about the issue, wherever we might be. He came up with the unexpected result that two-thirds favoured expansion into a new field of Visiting Fellowships, and only one-third an annexe and undergraduates.

The College was saved, by an outsider, and Sparrow always recognised it, candidly and generously. Much relieved, he went over to the majority. He had had a worrying time of it, and threatened that, if things went wrong, he would go back to London. (Was this course open to him?) Bridges was furious at the defeat, and tried to bully the Warden. 'If the scheme is not adopted *I shall be very angry.*' This had always worked in Whitehall. Not in All Souls. Here was where John's courage came into play. He merely commented, 'So what?'

Our greatest civil servant left the College, and never came into it again. This was a pity, and beneath his real greatness of character. No doubt he had more important things to do. In retirement he went on serving the country, in education, as Chancellor of Reading university, raising money for Oxford, etc. This was the second eminence who turned his back on the College in my time. The other was Radcliffe, no less eminent a man than Bridges. He kept in personal touch with Sparrow, on whom he had exercised an influence in encouraging perverseness, self-consciousness, posing. I kept in some touch with Radcliffe too. I went to stay with him at Stratford – just outside the park of the Lucys at Charlecote. He gave me his book, with its questioning title, *Not in Feather Beds* (from Sir Thomas More), with some College memories, but more of his Indian experience. He was a brilliant, sad man.

As for the young *enragé* in College, he would not take No for an answer. When there is a two-thirds majority, one has to accept the verdict. A German refugee whom we supported, got a university readership, then left us in the soup for America. Craster on this: 'He wouldn't take Yes for an answer.' I had supported the young Leftist's election, largely on his promise as a writer. He turned out no exemplar of loyalty, breaking his word to the Warden, and coming out in public in the press with the story of our internal affairs.

We were now free to go forward with the plan for Visiting Fellowships, more than meeting Oliver Franks's demands. In the course of the proceedings he came up to my rooms for my views. Taking him over to my big bookcase I demonstrated a whole shelf-full of my books; half of them College research into history – more literary books, like *A Cornish Childhood*, had been written at home in vacation. Oliver said, 'My dear Leslie, we all know that you do your research: what about the junior Fellows?' I did not feel called upon to defend them, and kept silence: not my business, but the Warden's. Some of them failed him. I'd have seen to it that they did their research!

We proceeded to carry out the Visiting Fellowships scheme on too generous a scale. It was vastly expensive. We purchased a property at Iffley containing a charming eighteenth-century house, and built an ugly block of flats which won – considering what the Sixties were – an architectural prize. Another block of flats was built in Crick Road. I never saw it: one lot was enough.

The plan was to accommodate fifteen Visiting Fellows a year – too many, if we were to maintain standards. One term I discovered that a happy academic from the north of Scotland took advantage of his opportunity to correct his O-level papers. I was affronted: that was not what the Visiting Fellowships were for. I watched with distaste his concentration on sopping up the College port: insensitive as such people are, he did not register that he was being observed by one who 'used to notice such things'. *L'homme moyen sensuel* again.

The scheme did better work as it got under way,

especially in bringing scholars from Russia, and other Slav countries. The whole point of the programme was to enable them to make use of the facilities of Oxford and to forward their work. The Russians had for so long been cut off from the outside world that they were apt to be incommunicable, unlike pre-war aristocrats, fluent in French and English. (Prince Yusupov, who assassinated Rasputin, had been at Christ Church; and I knew Prince Mirsky, who wrote a history of Russian literature, and was murdered under Stalin's auspices. At Cambridge I knew the eminent scientist Kapitza who, returning to Mother Russia, was never allowed out again.) In College I made friends with a bright young Polish lady, in my Elizabethan field, from the university of Lodz.

One eminent Polish scholar, the sociologist Kolakowski, we made a permanent Research Fellow. Since he was the leading, most sensible, authority on Marxism he and I had something in common. Both disillusioned – I at any rate had never set store by Marx's economics – we realised that there yet remained something retrievable in the collapse of a too systematised Marxism. There was the light he had thrown on the processes of history, the crucial importance of class-conflict – though indeed Aristotle had thought as much.

From Italy came an economist who was a protégé of Denis Mack Smith's, whom we adopted from Cambridge to be the leading historian of modern Italy. Since the likeable economist had Liberal illusions I felt free to tease him. Denis also was a liberal, though of a more sceptical hue. What price liberal illusions in Italy today? His scepticism was even stronger with regard to archbishops. As a tall choirboy at St Paul's he had had the privilege of carrying Lang's train, and was chagrined when, instead of receiving the customary half-a-crown, he was presented with a photograph of our Archbishop. This made him anti-clerical.

Here I take the opportunity to say that Lang did not care

tuppence about money. At Lambeth he lived like a prince of the Church with eleven indoor servants. When his few effects were transferred thither from College Woodward gave vent to his anti-clericalism by including Lang's cracked chamber-pot. Headlam, on a night of heavy bombing in London, met the Archbishop coming down the stairs of Lollards' Tower arrayed in his dressing gown – purple of course – and clutching his chamber-pot. 'When you arrive at my age you have need of this utensil.' He left the grandeur of Lambeth without a penny. Henson did better. He acquired a fine Suffolk manor house, and gave his address, up to fun as ever, as: 'H. Hensley Henson, Hintlesham Hall, Hipswich.' There I visited him only a fortnight before his death, indeed may have been responsible for it, for he had a weak heart and was so much excited to hear news of the College he loved.

What about the College's wider contacts?

In the eighteenth century the two Codrington governors of Barbados had founded Codrington College there. Earlier this century it had suffered badly from a fire; All Souls made a handsome contribution to its restoration. Now the Warden was invited over to give a lecture. What should he lecture about? Sparrow had no idea. I came up with an obvious subject, just right for him. In the eighteenth century the pre-eminent lawyer Blackstone, though not Warden, was the most famous member of the College. Blackstone's *Commentaries* formed the leading authority on English Law, a formative influence with the Founding Fathers of the American Constitution. It was a best-seller in his lifetime, and he made a fortune out of it. His portentous, robed figure, sculpted by Bacon, presides over one end of the Codrington Library. Blackstone had been not only a lawyer but a connoisseur, in those happy days; a good classic, he had also written verse, memorably 'The Lawyer's Farewell to his Muse'. This was an apt combination – what more appropriate for Warden Sparrow? He fell in with my suggestion and adopted it for his lecture on his visit to Barbados.

❊

John did well to bring back Penderel Moon, on his retirement from India and the World Bank, as estates bursar. Moon was an accomplished administrator and a practical farmer. He was also used to exercising authority, a high-minded moralist, careful about spending money. This was not popular with the new generation of junior Fellows. When the domestic bursarship became vacant the Warden proposed that the two offices should be united. This gave the young men their opportunity: they would not have Moon, and Sparrow gave way to them. Once more it was a case of taking the easier option. John said to me that Penderel did not regard the juniors with any sense of humour; evidently himself did not take them seriously. In effect he let his old friend down, a most remarkable man. Penderel resigned, and did not come back into College again, except occasionally to see me. It may have been a mistake to unite the two offices. The qualities required for the estates bursarship were quite different from those needed domestically, dealing with the College servants, for instance.

All Souls, which was built for forty Fellows, was now crowded – with sixty-five, and all those Visiting Fellows, including women. I was in favour of including them; it had been an inconvenience not to be able to invite women to ordinary meals. Formerly we had reserved this pleasure for a special 'Ladies' Night', once a term. Now the College was bulging at the seams. Gone were the old dignity and spaciousness; not only that, but the intimacy, the real friendship, the charm upon the beloved place. It was becoming more like anywhere else – though the same was happening all over Oxford. Democracy had broken in.

The cliché 'élitism' is a dirty word with the inferior, like the word 'racism' bandied about without rhyme or reason. I used to say to John that 'élitism' was a word used by the inferior to elide the difference between them and the superior. It was all part of the downward trend of standards everywhere and in everything. Only an élitist society has the respect of the elect. The people everywhere were obviously out of hand.

As for 'racism' we had a pretty experience of it in reverse; it made a comic episode. We elected a black from Ghana who would never have been elected if he had been white. He came in for the Fellowship as a philosopher; his papers were dubious, but as one can rarely tell if a philosopher is any good I asked Stuart Hampshire, conscientiously, whether it was all right to vote for him. Stuart gave a dubious 'Yes', and I gave him the benefit of the doubt. We were really voting against Apartheid in South Africa.

The servants had no objection to waiting on him. The Common Room man had nothing against him – 'The only thing is that when I come into the Common Room I can't *see* him.' This greatly amused John when I told him. In the dim irreligious light of night, semi-darkness, black dinner-jackets, our new Fellow melted into the mahogany. He next distinguished himself by making passes at the wives of other junior Fellows, and rented a house from one of them in North Oxford. Here he refused to pay the rent on the ground that the house was haunted by ghosts. He was not a success as a Fellow of All Souls. He shortly went back to darkest Africa, where he disappeared without trace under the benevolent rule of Nkrumah. Even the liberal-minded Hampshire – risen hope of the stern unbending Left – admitted that it had been a mistake to elect him.

Among the professorial Fellows recruited to us was the idiosyncratic figure of Evans-Pritchard, successor to Radcliffe-Brown in the chair of Social Anthropology. I had known E-P., as we called him, since undergraduate days

189

when he was rather a playboy. Something of this always remained with him, an attractive feature, and we were friends. Not disagreeably academic, or professionally professorial, he had had a wide experience in colonial Africa, which fitted him well for All Souls.

The anthropologists called this 'field-work', and it was notable how Radcliffe-Brown discounted the great Sir James George Frazer for not having done any. R-B. had done a little, when young, in the Andaman Islands – which did not put him, in my view, in the same class with Frazer, a formative influence on my mind when young. (I met him once in College with his bossy French wife.)

Evans-Pritchard had done more 'field-work' than any of them, both with the Senussi in Libya and father afield in the Sudan. In his day the Sudan was a model of British colonial administration, something to be proud of – like Nigeria under the rule of the exemplary Lugard. (One met him also in those great days, when everybody of any importance in public life turned up, sooner or later, at All Souls.) Evans-Pritchard was grieved at what happened to the Sudan when the British left – the massacres, the shambles, famine, all the good work undone. Well, of course.

E-P. was not of a marrying type, but was caught by one of his pupils. He said that he had been 'bewitched' and, to judge from his book on the Senussi, it seems that he shared their views on witchery, if not on witchcraft. He was regarded as the cat's whiskers as an anthropologist by his fellows the world over, and books were written about his work in his lifetime. Sympathetic as we were as fellow Celts, I could not share this cult. His views on history were puerile. A Roman convert from his adolescent Anglo-Catholicism, he believed the rubbish of Belloc and Chesterton about the English Reformation, about the character of Elizabeth I and the persecution of Catholics. (They at least survived, as Protestants did not in Spain.)

No better than Evelyn Waugh or Graham Greene on the subject – all of them Seconds or Thirds in the History School in my year. Why didn't they at least try to *learn*? The result was that I couldn't take E-P. seriously, intellectually speaking; nor, when I came to read the books about his work, could I see what it added up to. It read to me as if he were sceptical as to the subject himself.

In my view we were now over-balanced with academics, and too many Visiting Fellows. John would write to me at the Huntington Library hoping that I would be back at the College meeting in time to vote on his side. My vote was at his disposal. But I had been so inured to being defeated at every turn that I had become a devout defeatist. My vote wouldn't make any difference. John accepted things as they came, though the manciple told me that, after a defeat in College meeting, he would retire to the Lodgings, console himself with drink, and cry.[3] – As Pares's friend Roger Mynors cried bitterly when turned down for Master of Balliol, which he ought to have been. This had not been my reaction.

The sad thing was that All Souls was losing its uniqueness. There are all too many academic institutions in the modern world, far too many students out of hand and at the bottom of so many troubles, students' unions and what not. In the USA 'Education' is by far the largest industry, and professors ten a penny. In the old grand days at All Souls they were second-class citizens – and far less interesting than the grandees with their far-flung experience of the world, from whom one learned so much. In academe one could learn for oneself.

We still retained specimens from the larger world. My mate, now Lord Sherfield, had had a wide diplomatic experience, ending up as Ambassador in Washington, and

---

[3] At Downing College, Cambridge, after a meeting illuminated by the presence of F.R. Leavis, the Master would return to his Lodge, and make straight for the gin.

then shouldered duty as Chancellor of Reading university in succession to Bridges. We sported a Lord Chancellor in Hailsham, a Law Lord in Wilberforce, Cabinet Ministers in Douglas Jay and Keith Joseph. No bishops.

How about the future?

Three young men were in government. I had pushed hard for the election of Robert Jackson and John Redwood – Warden Sparrow rather unenthusiastic. William Waldegrave I had known since he presided over the Literary Society at Eton, which gave me an intelligent hearing (see above, p. 34) for my work in solving the problems of Shakespeare's Sonnets. John was curiously unsympathetic to elections from the School of English Literature, where again I pressed successfully for Andrew Harvey and Peter Conrad. Max Mallowan remarks in his Memoirs that he found Sparrow unsympathetic to his subject, archaeology, in which he had made rich discoveries in the Middle East. Anyway we elected him, as we had not the controversial Woolley, of the Biblical 'Ur of the Chaldees', whom Adams had proposed. Max and his wife, Agatha Christie, became dear friends of mine. I loved going out to lunch with them at Wallingford, where now they lie in the churchyard beneath the shadow of Cholsey church tower. I always look out for that church tower from the railway train into or out of Oxford, and remember them.

We did extend hospitality to two poets: Philip Larkin when he was working on his Book of Twentieth Century Verse in the Bodleian; and Auden when he left New York to settle back in Oxford. Wystan stayed with us for a month. His first night in College he was robbed of all the money in his wallet, and next morning he came to consult me. I said: 'My dear Wystan, didn't you sport your oak?' i.e. lock your door. No, he hadn't. In the old days, when we were undergraduates at the House, no one thought of locking doors. Today the world had changed, society was different – it was quite common for undergraduates to steal from each other.

Some young man, with wife and child, had taken advantage of Wystan's religiosity with a hard-luck story. Wystan wrote a cheque for him. The young man also took note of the convenient ground-floor rooms to come back again that night – Auden always went early to bed at 9 p.m. The young man had given his name and address, so could he have been guilty? He got off. It was a bad omen for Wystan's return to Oxford, which did not turn out well. When he died he was thinking of returning to America.

❁

My time in College was becoming short. One of our outside Fellows, who did nothing to remember him by, brought forward the proposition that Fellows should be retired – unlike Cambridge Fellows – at sixty-seven. In a crowded college that was reasonable, but it happened that I was the first upon whom the axe fell. Out! 'lock, stock, and barrel' as an uncongenial young lawyer put it. Two at least of the Fellows expressed their disapproval, even a sense of shock; they couldn't think of the College without the familiar figure who had been in evidence there since 1925.

It was John who mitigated this sentence of exclusion (Trevor-Roper kindly wanted to make a case of it – anything to disparage All Souls). My Fellowship was extended, exceptionally, to the age of seventy. During those three years I plodded away in the Bodleian, until in going into Simon Forman's papers in depth – E.K. Chambers had only skimmed the surface – I discovered the Dark Lady of the Sonnets, just where she should be: to my surprise, and everybody else's, though even more to their annoyance. Nobody, in all the centuries before, had spotted her existence, though my friend John Buxton knew her long poem, *Salve Deus Rex Judaeorum*. He had refused to accept all the preliminary steps which I had firmly established in my previous research work at the Huntington. If they had not been absolutely correct I should not have been led on to the identification of Emilia Bassano, the musical and promiscuous Mrs Lanier. Professor Kirsch of the university of California came with me to the Bodleian to inspect the manuscripts. He said, 'I wonder how many more centuries we should have had to wait before the right combination of scholarship and perception found the answer.'

Funnily enough, John Sparrow was not best pleased. A little grain of the early envy emerged. We went through it together, John putting every possible objection – the 'lawyer in literature' again – picking up all the minutiae, the hand-writing. He did not appreciate the complete consistency of characters, historical and topical circumstances, the crucial dating, as an historian would. It is not unfair to say that he had little imagination and, clever as he was, he was not intuitively perceptive. In the end he came round, and saw that it could not but be – no other answer was possible, and there never has been any answer to the discovery, nor ever will be.

I might go so far as to claim that I earned my last three years in College, and our relations became closer and closer, when I returned as a Quondam, i.e. former Fellow. Shortly we were given the title of emeritus. That did not console me: I wrote a poem about the *revenant*, whose footsteps could feel their way up the steps and along my corridor to those familiar rooms. I never entered them again. (As Lang, after his retirement, never went back to Cuddesdon.)

John remained faithful to his old studies: the Classics, particularly Latin verse, law, and English literature. To History he gave the benefit of the doubt, for he knew no English history. So, as we sat together at the head of the table at dessert he liked me to tell him stories of the past. He felt that now he knew the difference between Richard II and Richard III. As he had not a good memory, and I had

194

almost total recall, I used to repeat stories and episodes to amuse him.

What he liked were *mots* that had some sharp point to them, of sarcasm or malice. Of Charles I's time somebody asked: 'What do the Arminians hold?' Answer: 'All the best bishoprics and deaneries in England.' He worked at his own wit, not a natural wit like that of his old mentor, Maurice Bowra, who made him his literary executor. John would say: 'What will remain of the works of a man whose prose is unreadable and his verse unpublishable?' Maurice's prose is not unreadable, but he left two volumes of pornographic verse.

John did his best for Simon, so faithful to the College, though nobody loved him. Again John and I were at one in not disliking him. He was High Steward of the university, an office in which our Wilberforce succeeded him. His overlarge portrait had been removed from Hall, in some re-arrangement of pictures. Sparrow had the happy idea of having his coat-of-arms sculpted in stone on one of the Hawksmoor towers in the inner quad. There it is, high up with its heraldic supporters and absurd device: 'J'ai ain*si mon* nom.' When he came to die he was coffined in his scarlet robes as Doctor of Civil Law. Perhaps, like President Jefferson, in the end he valued academic more than political honours.

❁

The time had come for Sparrow's retirement, and the College was fortunate to elect Sir Patrick Neill. Here again was a lawyer of the old school, with experience of public affairs as head of the Press Council, but a dynamo of energy. Soon it became again our turn to provide the Vice-Chancellor for the university, and Pat Neill's term of office is already historic. It is as if the College were making up for lost time and he were a permanent Vice-Chancellor,

195

a full-time job, so hard at work he needed a deputy in College. He set on foot the world-fund to meet the new needs of Oxford at large, and travelled all over the world to promote it.

The College treated the ex-Warden handsomely. He had the double set of rooms in the Georgian house at Iffley to himself, plenty of space, a rose-garden beneath his windows. But it was not space enough for his now enormous collections of books, prints, water-colours, and I doubt if he ever acclimatised himself to life at Iffley after a longer spell in the Lodgings than any Warden since Anson. *That* was his home. When back in Oxford I would occasionally go down to see him – not many did, as the manciple predicted they would not.

An exception was John Simmons, the admirable and expert bibliographer whom Sparrow had made Librarian – one of the best appointments he ever made. For this was his chosen field, his earliest love from a schoolboy, as Kenneth Clark describes him at Winchester. Simmons was a faithful attendant, and those two could mull over their book-lore, and plan the disposition of what had become perhaps the finest private collection of the time, except for Geoffrey Keynes's, another of John's book-buddies.

In his last years Sparrow gave a series of broadcasts, *Words on the Air*, concise, reflective, salutary – if only they were listened to, as of course they were not, in the squalid society of today into which we had survived. With lawyerly moderation he tried to make allowances for it, offered compromises, made qualifications – as I would not. I had no use for it – and had the past at my disposal. John's title bore a characteristic innuendo: of course his words, every one of which I agreed with, were lost *on the air*. It is odd that in the end he should have become something of a *guru*, salutary but of course unheeded.

He also published a collection of his verses and epigrams. He was an accomplished writer of verse – not at all the

196

same thing as writing poetry. At last, relegated to loneliness at Iffley, he wrote a real poem, 'A Day with Myself'. He was much pleased when I wrote to tell him so. Some verses described what he thought of himself – and others too, not quite fairly:

> Here, with his talents in a napkin hid,
> Lies one who much designed, and nothing did;
> Postponing and deferring, day by day,
> He quite procrastinated life away,
> And, when at length the summons came to die,
> With his last breath put off – mortality.

That was not quite fair to himself, for it represented the pose which frustrated his gifts. Though a gifted man, he accomplished nothing big, in books or life. He one day said, generously, to me, 'You are creative, I am not. I don't want anything – except to manoeuvre people a bit about the board.' He was good at that, and made a good Warden – the College had been right, as usual, to choose him – internally, if not altogether externally.

What was the clue to what people considered a curiously frustrated personality? My diagnosis of the case was simple. Underneath the carefully constructed pose his inner nature was feminine, sensitive and sentimental. At New College he had been put through the logic-chopping machine of H.W.B. Joseph. Some people took to this naturally – notably Moon, Herbert Hart, Roy Harrod and, to a lesser extent, Douglas Jay. With John Sparrow it was superimposed upon his real nature. At the Bar this was reinforced by the influence of Radcliffe, who also encouraged the perverseness. In time this dried up the inner juices, from which inspiration comes.

It was clean contrary to my gospel, which was, and is, that one should develop one's inner nature to the fullest of which it is capable, not cut across it and frustrate it.

197

Self-consciousness is the enemy of creativeness.

John was now visibly failing, and allowed people to see it. Drink was catching up on him, as with so many Public School boys. I could not understand it, or tried to. As adolescents it was thought a 'good thing' to know about wine, a proper social accoutrement. I used to watch, with distaste, if not contempt, a young man making a to-do with sniffing the *bouquet* of the College wine. Geoffrey Faber once reproached me: 'My dear Leslie, you don't know what you are missing.' It then transpired that he didn't know whether what he was drinking was claret or burgundy. I thought it a silly cult, and the decanters twice around with the dessert quite sufficient, not half-a-dozen times.

When John came up from his exile to dine he was now faltering, sometimes already sozzled. I came back sometimes, gownless as a Quondam – I made a point of that; John's gown in tatters, a disgrace. I would take him by the arm, after all his senior, lead him off the dais, and pilot him into Common Room. There I could keep him under control, deliberately telling him stories, jokes, to keep him off the drink. He was getting out of control, and those last years were sad. His driving licence was taken away, after an awkward incident. He was marooned at Iffley and, when he did come into dinner, behaved badly. The Common Room took an unprecedented step, and debarred him from coming. I thought this improper for a former Warden and, rather upset, wrote in to protest. When he was bedridden, or in and out of nursing homes, I used to send him coloured post-cards to keep in touch.

When he died I was more affected than I expected. Away in Cornwall I kept thinking of him – after all, so much had happened between him and me over so many years – I could not think of the College without him. His last words to me were, 'I cannot tell you how much I admire you.' And then, 'Pray for me.' I could have wept. Was he, after all, more generous to me than I to him?

7. *Warden Sparrow*

I did not think of writing a formal poem in his memory, but at home in Cornwall, beyond going back to Oxford, I kept missing him so much *in mind*, that a simple little poem wrote itself, almost without thinking. Here it is.

John Sparrow

He is gone. The spirit of the place
Lived in him: the rooms are redolent
Of him. I see him bent over his books,
Or offering them to his guests to sniff the vellum,
An addict of good binding, paper, print;
Or yet again stealthily prowling his lawn
To snip the heads of roses when hardly blown;
Hear him in chapel reciting the Founder's prayer
With musical voice and well-considered air.
I see him move archly across the grass
Through the gate and make his way along
To his loved private quarters, the Lodgings;
Or sipping coffee beneath Hawksmoor's towers
On summer evenings after dinner, looking
Across to the dome of the Radcliffe Camera.
Alas, no more those pleasant interludes
Under the chestnut trees of the Warden's garden
Exchanging academic jokes with friends,
Emerging from Anson's and Sumner's mausoleum
Which John reserved, he said, 'to sack the Fellows' –
Really a gloomy den piled high with books,
Accumulated bibliophily,
While he lived blithe and free above,
Confronting his old Wykehamist college
Whence we elected him, a precocious boy,
Broad brow, falling lick of hair, firm chin,
Always alert to be amused, a quip
Ready on lip, and intermittent charm.

199

All Souls

Evening, and the questioning of birds.
A bugle blows an erotic note over the city,
Light creeps round to the north face of the tower,
Grey stone chimneys are still and void of life.
Here is neither marrying nor giving in marriage,
No heart to hold nor limbs to cherish.
The happy birds go winging on their business,
Soldiers in the street on theirs.
Beyond the walls, the roofs and eaves,
Than walls of stone or bars of iron more binding
These intellectual integuments, because self-willed.

Mullioned windows of the Middle Age
Look blindly out upon a world they do not know,
Gargoyles express their child-like humour
Propitiate the powers of evil, fear of the unknown.
A figure of Christ stands up on his perch
With didactic gesture of hand and parted hair.

The shadow of the tower moves along the roof;
A clatter of cups and plates in the lodge
Speaks of domestic content, and marks the hour.

Later, high-flying swifts sweep the sky,
Cry their passionate unsatisfied cry,
Aspire about the waiting, watching city,
Emblems of incurable nostalgia of the heart.

(1930s)

The Choice

O look at the apple blossom, buds of May
That dress with white and glimmering array
The lawns of Spring at this moment of evening;
O look at the lemon-green of lime, gold beech, dark
    yew,
Plumes of poplars that wave and lean to the East.
O Life, World, Time, if only one might arrest this
    moment!
But time moves on into a world that knows one not.

Look now upon this other side:
The formal magnificence, the Roman world of stone,
The dome with its volutes and urns,
This learned prison, the walls that shut me in,
This cemetery with its ordered monuments.

Like a madman I go from one side to the other,
Look out upon this scene and now on that,
Avid of life, by fever of mind possessed,
Poised like the frozen eagle for the unknown,
Confront the formal West, turned like him to stone.

                         (1940s)

All Souls Night in Wyoming

The saddle-back hills and cattle millionaires
Of Omaha are a November night away:
I wake to find the country white with frost,
Snow-fences already up along the track.

201

All Souls in My Time

We're in Wyoming and, high up, shortly stop
At Laramie of the old Oregon Trail:
Beside the station a dainty yellow coach
Used in Yellowstone in earlier days.
All night we have been slowly climbing up
To this bare plateau, snow-mist over uplands,
Nothing in sight but cattle and icy streams,
Nothing but the ghosts of vanished Indians,
A hawk planes over the wastes, here and there
A house huddles beside the railroad track.
The long slow reptile of the train winds round
A bluff, piñons holding to the living rock.

This is Rock Springs, an arctic settlement
Of miners, seeking gold and drilling oil.
Green River, a platform swept by bitter wind:
I scurry to the warm station-hall and return
With *The Quiet American*. Onward we go
Through driving sleet and vagrant snow that shuts
Out all but the vicinity of railroad sidings,
Disused coaches, metal containers, huts.
Now over the Continental Divide the ground
Is free of snow: haystacks stand in meadows,
Some trees and ragged willows flushed with red;
Overhead, a flight of mallard from the lake.
At Soda Springs, a desolate hard-bitten spot
With stores for Stockmen's Hardware, Groceries,
The bars and dives that nourish their hardened lives.

As day draws in, I see a different scene:
Candles lit in a dark panelled room
Flicker in the pools of mahogany,
Firelight on coved ceiling, a bust of Wren
Looking serene on the familiar gathering;
The glasses are filled with wine, the feast wears on.
This is All Souls' Night. The great Christ Church bell

202

And many a lesser bell sound through the room.
Perhaps a ghost may come, for it is a ghost's right.
I eat the bread of voluntary exile:
Alone in this wilderness I celebrate.

(1950s)

All Souls Day

Justorum animae in manu dei sunt.
Brightly, warmly descends the autumn sun
On the morning chapel, and it is All Souls day.
The shadow of a bird passes up the painted
Glass, even as our lives in time will pass –
Colours on reredos and rows of the dead,
Amethyst and saffron, rose, blue, green.
Here they are gathered in mind who all are gone.

The ancient Warden reads the Founder's prayer,
Silvery hair, grey eyes, clean-shaven face,
His 'Pembers' a tuft of hair on each suave cheek.
Sermon by Henson, of beetling eyebrows
And clacking teeth, hissing across to Lang
How his predecessor at Durham, 'Analogy' Butler,
Had refused the primacy for 'he would not be
A pillar of a declining Church': on me
Not lost, for he wanted the see of York.
Old Oman whom Henson reproved for being late,
'Not only for the General Confession but
The Absolution you most stand in need of.'

Quavering-voiced, sharp-tongued Johnson, chaplain
And hunting parson, who closed discussion with
'Never ask for anything, never refuse anything,
And never resign anything' – wrestling with Morrah's

203

All Souls in My Time

Soul, bent on going over to Rome:
Whose panegyric Reggie Harris preached
Improbably in Westminster Cathedral.
Reggie moves out, birdlike, head on one side:
I think of his jokes,
Handel, 'the great master of the common chord'.
Carcassonne, 'Violé par Le Duc.'

They all move up in seniority
To make their offering at the altar.
Robertson, sharp of nose and kind of heart,
Loquacity his only vice. And now
Comes Geoffrey Dawson of the *Times*,
Of fatal influence on foreign policy,
With his friend the 'Prophet' Curtis, who had
A message for the world, but lost his way.
Another, wounded by loss in a later war.

Behold Spencer Wilkinson in spats
Shuffling with myopic gait up the steps,
Who'd have one think he had enjoyed the favours
Of Sarah Bernhardt: soft of heart:
A military man, marsh-mallow within.
MacGregor, muttering to himself, having
Been blown up on the Menin Road –
That earlier war,
Began the ruin of the age in which we live.

Woodward served in Salonica; see him
With sceptical smile and clerical trail,
Approach the communion rail.
Bridges, of frosty eye and intellect,
Secrets of state well down 'in the deep, deep freeze'.

Pares, at whose election the Warden dreamed
Primus inter pares:

204

On whose beloved head cruel fate
Fell, unable to move muscle or limb.
Summer afternoons we'd sit beneath
The whitebeam's canopy and watch the sky
Wheeling over battlement and spire,
While time ate up the precious hour.

They all served Church or State in their day
Who now are here, shrouded in surplices
As once they were, and now are ghosts, alive
Only in the dedicated mind.
November sunlight flickers across the aisle,
Falls upon stall and altar, whereon
The candles shed their flame, and it is written:
The souls of the just are in the hand of God.

(1960s)

The 'Revenant'

The door opens to the familiar key,
And once more I am within the rooms
Formerly my own, no longer mine.
I am a stranger. Yet so much of life
Passed within these walls, so much
Happiness in work, looking up to see
Gold and black caverns in the copper beech,
Rose-flush of dawn upon the Camera,
Moonlight upon the dome sifted with snow,
So much too, of anguish and waiting.

My feet echo along the empty corridor,
Here are the bookshelves that held my books,
Gaping windows that leave all exposed –
The familiar ghost, unwanted *revenant*.

All Souls in My Time

Floorboards quicken to my faithful feet,
Send back an unacquainted sound.

Nothing has changed. Yet all has changed:
Some spirit has flown, gone out of things,
Leaving untouched a glimpse of the garden
From my bedroom of secret memories,
Of illness and intermittent happiness.
Autumn is evident in the garden-beds,
Rain on Michaelmas daisies, lemon-gold
Of leaves and bedraggled flowers.

It is All Souls day, when we pray
For those who were here before us and felt
Perhaps as I do today. A bell tolls
Its reminiscent note: Remember them,
The souls of the faithful departed
Who once lived here and had their being
Even as I. The door clangs behind me –
I could tell its sound two hundred miles away;
My feet recall the tread of the stone stairs:
I could find my way blindfold,
Who now go down for the last time
And out of the door, for ever, away.

(1970s)

Index of Names

Index of Names

Le Bon, Gustave, 180
Lee, R.W., 27, 96
Lewis, C.S., 36, 139
Lipson, E., 47
Lloyd George, David, 99, 115, 165
Lothian, Lord, 128
Lowell, Lawrence, 180

Macartney, C.A., 116-17
MacDonald, Ramsay, 79, 86-7, 92, 99
MacDowell, A.S., 23
MacGregor, D.H., 22, 46, 100
Mack Smith, Denis, 186
Madan, Geoffrey, 103-4
Mair, Mrs, 111
Maitland, F.W., 182
Makins, Roger, Lord Sherfield, 20, 25, 62, 73, 82, 129
Malcolm, Sir Dougal, 85, 157
Mallowan, Sir Max, 192
Mamoulian, Rouben, 177-8
Mary, Queen, 97
Mathew, David, 96
Mathew, Gervase, 54, 96
Maugham, W. Somerset, 173
Maurois, André, 160
Mayow, John, 46

McFarlane, K.B., 20, 114-15, 123, 148, 179
McManners, John, 36
Mengs, Raphael, 42, 176
Milner, Lord, 78, 81, 84, 99
Molotov, V.M., 92
Moltke, Helmut von, 124
Moon, Sir Penderel, 21, 25, 34, 93-4, 188, 197
Morrah, Sir Dermot, 32, 43, 55-6, 86
Morrell, Lady Ottoline, 22
Morris, Sir William, 63, 71
Muggeridge, Malcolm, 20
Müller, Max, 150
Murray, Sir Charles Augustus, 67
Mussolini, Benito, 101-2, 119
Mynors, Sir Roger, 191

Namier, Sir Lewis, 112, 118

Neale, Sir J.E., 133
Nehru, Jawaharlal, 94
Neill, Sir Patrick, 195
Nicolson, Sir Harold, 104, 122, 126

Oman, Sir Charles, 19, 31, 38-9, 47, 51, 58, 70, 93, 102, 144, 150, 152, 154
O'Neill, Con, 98, 141

Pantin, W.A., 20
Pares, Richard, 21, 23, 29, 34, 44, 47, 69, 72, 76, 100, 102-3, 107-8, 110-14, 117, 119, 149, 152
Pares, Sir Bernard, 108
Pattison, Mark, 174
Pember, F.W., 14, 25, 27, 35, ch. 2 *passim*, 125-6, 155, 173, 175
Perosa, Alessandro, 173
Philby, Kim, 95
Pimlott, Ben, 119
Pius X, 96
Pius XI, 96
Plamenatz, John, 138
Plunket, Sir Horace, 108-9
Pollard, A.F., 45, 53, 57
Potter, Beatrice, 44
Power, Eileen, 111
Powicke, Sir F.M., 144
Prothero, Rowland, Lord Ernle, 106-7
Pryce Jones, Alan, 161

Quiller Couch, Sir Arthur, 37

Radakrishnan, Sir S., 94-5
Radcliffe, Lord, 17, 25, 41, 63, 69, 75, 80, 84, 94, 169-70, 184
Radcliffe-Brown, A.R., 47, 116, 190
Raleigh, Sir Thomas, 93
Ramsden, W., 65
Redwood, John, 192
Rees, Goronwy, 95, 116, 133-7, 157, 162-5
Reith, Lord, 35
Rickett, Sir Denis, 20
Robbins, Lord, 52, 101, 112, 158, 178

210

211

Prize Fellows
1925-1974

1925

A.L. Rowse (Christ Church)
R.M. Makins (Christ Church)

1926

G.F. Hudson (Queen's)
A.H.M. Jones (New College)

1927

E.P. Moon (New College)
D.S. Dannreuther (Balliol)

1928

H.V. Hodson (Balliol)
A.H. Campbell (University)

1929

D.H.F. Rickett (Balliol)
J.H.A. Sparrow (New College)

1930

D.P.T. Jay (New College)

1931

M.G. Rees (New College)
Hon. Q.M. Hogg (Christ Church)

1932

I. Berlin (Corpus Christi)
D.A.P. Reilly (New College)
R.O. Wilberforce (New College)

1933

J.L. Austin (Balliol)

1934

J.E.C. Hill (Balliol)
R.T.E. Latham (Magdalen)

1935

A.D. Woozley (Queen's)
C.D.W. O'Neill (Balliol)

1936

S.N. Hampshire (Balliol)
D.A. Routh (New College)

1937

A.J. Brown (Queen's)
A.D.M. Cox (Hertford)

Prize Fellows 1925–1974

1938

R.d'O. Butler (Balliol)
H.W. Davies (Balliol)
J.E.S. Fawcett (New College)

1946

L.H. Butler (Magdalen)
H.A.P. Fisher (Christ Church)

1947

A.J. Holladay (Trinity)

1948

J.P. Cooper (Magdalen)
I.M.D. Little (New College)

1949

A.M. Quinton (Christ Church)

1950

F.P. Neill (Magdalen)
J.L. Bullard (Magdalen)
M.A.E. Dummett (Christ Church)

1951

R.L. Wade-Gery (New College)
B.A.O. Williams (Balliol)

1952

D.L. Edwards (Magdalen)
A.W. Tyson (Magdalen)

1953

P.S. Lewis (Magdalen)
C.J. Morse (New College)

1954

No Election

1955

K.V. Thomas (Balliol)
G.L. Huxley (Magdalen)

1956

P.R.L. Brown (New College)
C.M. Taylor (Balliol)

1957

J.J.L. Wolfenden (Magdalen)
J.F. Lever (University)

1958

F.G.B. Millar (Trinity)

1959

J.D. Caute (Wadham)
W.E. Abraham (University)
A.G.S. Clayre (Christ Church)

1960

F.M. Hope (New College)
Hon. N.A.O. Lyttelton (Magdalen)

213

Prize Fellows 1925–1974

1961

R.R. Stuart (Wadham)
M. Lipton (Balliol)

1962

M.D. Deas (New College)
E.L. Hussey (New College)

1963

Hon. C.J. Makins (New College)

1964

R. Briggs (Balliol)

1965

E.J. Mortimer (Balliol)

1966

R.M. Franklin (Christ Church)
J.L.H. Thomas (Balliol)

1967

D.A. Parfit (Balliol)
J.C. Clarke (Wadham)

1968

R.V. Jackson (St Edmund Hall)
S.R.L. Clark (Balliol)

1969

C.P. Wormald (Balliol)
C.J.G. Wright (Trinity)

1970

M.C.C. Hart (Magdalen)
P.J. Conrad (New College)

1971

N.S.R. Hornblower (Balliol)
Hon. W.A. Waldegrave (Corpus
    Christi)

1972

J.A. Redwood (Magdalen)
R.H.A. Jenkyns (Balliol)

1973

A.C. Harvey (Exeter)

1974

L.D.J. Henderson (Balliol)